BP Shipping Pictorial

BP Shipping Pictorial

The Golden Years 1945–1975

Ray Solly

Whittles Publishing

Whittles Publishing Ltd.,
Dunbeath,
Caithness, KW6 6EG,
Scotland, UK

www.whittlespublishing.com

ISBN 978-184995-474-7

Printed and bound in the UK
by Halstan Printing Group, Amersham.

CONTENTS

The author

Dr Ray Solly enjoyed a first career as a navigating officer in the Merchant Navy, serving aboard deep-sea dry cargo vessels and supertankers plus, during the long vacations whilst studying, in the engagingly different lifestyle of chief or second mate aboard coasters. He spent 20 years as a residential schoolmaster in two independent schools, during which time he moonlighted by teaching coastal navigation and radar courses in the School of Maritime Operations at HMS *Dryad*. Following voluntary redundancy, a third professional career has evolved as a marine author. In these more recent years, he has been commissioned and contracted by publishers and maritime organisations to research and write technical and historical non-fiction books, plus over 30 associated articles for shipping magazines.

www.raysollyseabooks.com

By the same author:
Supertankers: Anatomy and Operation (Witherby, 2001)
Picturesque Harbours (Frith, 2002)
Gravesend: A History of Your Town (Frith, 2002)
Mariner's Launch (Whittles, 2005)
BP Shipping: A Group Fleet History (Chatham, 2005)
Mariner's Voyage (Whittles, 2008)
Athel Line: A Fleet History (History Press, 2009)
Nothing over the Side: Examining Safe Crude Oil Tankers (Whittles, 2010)
Manual of Tanker Operations (Brown, Son & Ferguson, 2011)
Mariner's Rest (Whittles, 2012)
BP's Early Large Tankers: Ships and Life Aboard (Ships Illustrated, 2015)
Questing for the Dove: A Spiritual Journey (Lighthouse Christian – USA, 2018)
The Development of Crude Oil Tankers: A Historical Miscellany (Pen and Sword, 2021)
Tate and Lyle's Secret Navy: The Athel Line (Whittles, in preparation)
Living the River Thames (Whittles, in preparation)

Acknowledgements

I am grateful to those who have helped by providing photographs supporting this book: A. Duncan, Aalborg Proactive, the BP Archive at University of Warwick, C. van Noort, C.L. Reynolds, Captain 'Tinker' Taylor, Fotoship, G. Brownell, J. Prentice, M. Cass, M. Dippy, M. Lennon, N. Cutts, Roly Weekes, the Sir Joseph Isherwood Society, Skyfotos, *Tanker and Bulk Carrier* magazine, *Tanker Times* magazine, *The Motor Ship* magazine, and the World Ship Society Photographic Library.

Introduction

Among the seafaring community until probably the 1970s BP Shipping was known colloquially as BTC. This nickname originated from the initials on the early funnels representing the British Tanker Company. But to appreciate how the shipping arm of the parent Anglo-Persian company developed from modest beginnings in 1915 to become a world-famous conglomerate running VLCCs and assorted product carriers 60 years later necessitates a brief look at some early developments in design and construction of the basic tanker.

In November 1861, two years after the momentous discovery of commercially viable quantities of oil in Pennsylvania, the brig *Elisabeth Watts*, laden with over 1,300 barrels of crude oil and kerosene, sailed from the Delaware River to the Thames. The ships that followed her were initially known as 'oil carrying vessels', and although progress in oil carrier developments was slow at first, it was inexorable. So it was not too long before necessity fermented ideas in the minds of enterprising men to build progressively towards developing a class of ship which would become the 'tanker'. It was not too long, either, before the heavy crude oil was found too viscous for ordinary uses, so became refined into either 'dirty oils' such as fuel to fire the boilers of ships and other means of transport, and 'products', under whose umbrella would be included paraffin and 'motor spirit' – assorted ranges of diesel and gas oils.

In 1863, the sailing vessel *Atlantic* was built. She had an iron hull with one long continuous centreline oil-tight longitudinal bulkhead, fitted with three transversal bulkheads to give a total of eight cargo tanks, carrying a total of 700 tons of oil. The vessel was not a success, but she paved the way for greater improvements in the by now earnest search for a purpose-designed ship that would carry greater quantities of crude oil safely across the turbulently rough Atlantic waters.

It was 20 years later, in 1885, that the British Newcastle-based shipbuilder Armstrong Mitchell (later to become Swan Hunter and Wigham Richardson), was approached by Wilhelm Riedemann's German-American Oil Company to construct a ship to carry its crude oil cargoes. The task appealed to the imagination of Colonel Henry Swan, a director of the builders, who designed *Glückauf*, a motorised sailing ship which became the prototype upon which all subsequent tankers, albeit with considerable modifications, would be based. According to the imperial system of measurements prevalent at the time, the tanker was 310 feet long by 37.3 feet in the beam. She was built according to Samuel Plimsoll's load line system, introduced in 1876, to transport 3,000 deadweight tons on her summer line (sdwt), with a gross registered tonnage (grt) of 2,307 and a moulded depth of 31 feet. *Glückauf* was launched on 16 June 1886 and sailed almost immediately on her maiden voyage.

Not regarding her modest capacity, *Glückauf* was innovative in a number of ways. Whilst she retained the single oil-tight longitudinal bulkhead, this was single-angled and double-riveted, and was fitted with eight transversals to give a greater number of tanks than those in *Atlantic*. A fore-and-aft expansion trunk was constructed to each tank in a tween-deck, with bulkheads on either side, which increased cargo capacity, allowing the tanks to be loaded to the full. Additional space was consequently provided either for extra cargo or for bunkers, with a major contribution made towards reducing free-surface area 'sloshing' effects.

Whilst the bridge remained midships, the engines were placed aft, with a separating cofferdam fitted, containing the pump room. The then customary double bottom below the cargo tanks was eliminated, which allowed oil to fill the entire cargo space. This was also a major contribution to safety, for it eliminated the hydrocarbon gas leaks into the engine space that had previously caused a number of explosions. The potential loss of strength to the hull was compensated by a system of angles spread across the bottom of the ship at regular intervals. Her shell plating was constructed partly of steel and partly of iron, giving additional strengthening to the hull and allowing a previously unknown degree of elasticity when the vessel pitched and rolled in heavy seas.

Electric lighting was provided in officers' accommodation aft and in the generous crew quarters for'ard, as well as in other useful areas, and also for the navigation lights. This increased the efficiency of the masthead lights in particular, eliminating the slightly yellow tinge that had been so much a feature of the previous oil lamps. Her triple-expansion steam engine gave her a service speed of 10 knots. The sails with which she was fitted did not prove very successful, and the tanker was far from perfect, but she continued in service until 1893, when she ran aground off Fire Island, just outside New York, to be declared a constructive total loss.

In 1909 the innovative oil company Shell Tankers introduced a system of summer tanks into its ships. This important development enabled tankers to carry oil across different temperate zones whilst on regular passages. When crude oil was loaded into tankers it could not fill the complete cargo tank so was loaded only to 98 per cent capacity. This allowed the ship to sail on passage between oceans to ports in hotter or colder countries that those where the oil had been loaded, causing it either to expand or contract. The tanks also contributed towards reducing the perennial problem of helping solve free-surface area reduction in each tank.

The next milestone towards creating a ship upon which later vessels would be constructed was also designed by one of those names who, like Henry Swan, are destined to live perpetually in the comparative niche world of commercial oil-tanker markets. Joseph Isherwood (or 'Sir' as he became) was a surveyor to Lloyd's Register of Shipping in London for 11 years between 1896 and 1907. He then took advantage of an opportunity

The British-built 3,000 sdwt *Glückauf* was the first tanker that helped provide solutions to the ongoing problems of free-surface effects which created dangerous 'sloshing' effects, affecting the stability of the ship when in beam seas. Eliminating the double bottom prevented leakage of hydrocarbon gases into the engine room and accommodation areas. She was in service from 1886 until 1893 and proved a prototype tanker upon which further design ideas were created. World Ship Society.

to develop his ideas in private practice, which allowed him to focus in greater depth on public concerns regarding ship safety. His applications paid more dividends than he could have originally conceived. Isherwood developed advances made since the *Glückauf* by retaining the single longitudinal bulkhead and transversals, but introduced a series of bottom brackets between an interlocking of longitudinal and transversal girders fitted with short vertical stiffeners that strengthened the internal cargo tanks. He extended his transversal frames from the hull shell plating with horizontal stiffeners that formed the expansion trunk.

Isherwood's design was revolutionary. He had reduced the number of transversals in each tank and introduced far stronger web plates that were reinforced with corner brackets and a series of longitudinal girders extending along the shell plating and expansion trunk areas. A stronger ship emerged that served as a model for later developments, which was immediately adopted for both dry cargo vessels and tankers.

Not surprisingly, as a result of Isherwood's work tanker developments did not stand still. Inevitably, his ideas produced a range of tankers worldwide that increased in both size and cargo capacity. For example, by 1919 the British company Eagle Oil was working a tanker called *San Florentino* which was 18,000 sdwt, whilst the United States company Standard Oil just two years later had ordered two tankers, *William Rockefeller* and *John D. Archbold*, each of which bordered on approximately 23,000 sdwt, with an overall length of 572 feet and a beam of 75 feet.

Sir Joseph Isherwood remains heralded as one of the great names and innovators of oil-tanker design. His contribution towards tanker safety, with later modifications, remains recognised to this day in the modern very large and ultra large crude oil tankers. The Sir Joseph Isherwood Society.

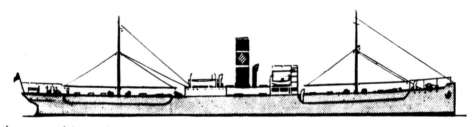

The 6,600 sdwt, 355.2-foot long, and 49.4-foot beam tanker *Paul Paix* was built in the British yards of Craggs in Middlesbrough, and soon proved the efficacy of Isherwood's revolutionary design. She was intended initially for carriage of 'motor spirits', but soon proved her versatility across the full gambit of oil cargoes. The vessel remained in service until 1930, when she was broken up.

Around 1923 Shell Tankers abolished summer tanks and replaced these with twin longitudinal bulkheads. This idea soon caught on, and later tankers transferred to the new tank configuration. The idea of twin longitudinals had been introduced previously to the tanker industry in 1916 with the Norwegian-owned 7,200 sdwt tanker *Hamlet*. She had been built in Gothenburg at the Götaverken yards. For some unknown reason, like so many ideas, the enhanced strengthened hull which also increased seagoing operational stability qualities was not universally accepted: this was surprising, bearing in mind that reduced operating costs transpired, opening markets more widely for the carriage of multi-grade crude oil cargoes.

ONE

The state of the BP fleet until 1939

In 1917 the British Tanker Company (BTC) took delivery of its first owned tanker, *British Emperor*. She was the first of the seven ships that formed the foundations of its later fleet. The tanker was 5,500 sdwt on an overall length of 345 feet, with a beam of 49.1 feet, and moulded depth 25.6 feet. She was launched from the Newcastle yards of Armstrong Whitworth on 18 February 1916, and completed in August the following year, when she immediately entered service on her maiden voyage. The vessel had one triple-expansion engine of 1,900 bhp, and was fitted with seven main port and starboard cargo tanks, a summer tank and a cargo hold for'ard.

BTC's first owned ship was the *British Emperor*, launched in 1916 and seen here alongside its second owned tanker, *British Empress*, launched the following year. This 5,500 sdwt vessel served the company until 7 May 1941, when on a voyage from Durban to Abadan she ran foul of the German merchant raider *Penguin* and was sunk some 300 miles SSE of Socotra. World Ship Society.

British Aviator, built in 1924, was the first company tanker to be powered by an oil engine. The 10,762 sdwt ship was built by Palmer's shipyard in Newcastle-upon-Tyne, and her 6-cylinder 3,435 bhp engine was also constructed by this firm, giving a service speed around 10.58 knots on a summer draught of 26.5 feet. The vessel continued in service until 1953, when she was demolished at Newport. *The Motor Ship*.

Over the years, the company gradually increased both the size and the capacity of its tanker fleet. By 1931, for example, it owned or managed 90 *British*-prefixed vessels and was competing favourably in both deep-sea and coastal oil trades.

BP Shipping's first motor ship, introduced in 1924, was the 10,762 sdwt *British Aviator*, built on the Isherwood system by Palmer's Shipbuilding Company in Newcastle. The tanker, 439.8 feet overall length, 57.1 feet beam and moulded depth 33.8 feet, was completed in August of that year. She was fitted with a 6-cylinder oil engine manufactured by the builders with an output of 4,925 bhp at 90 rpm geared to a single propeller shaft, giving her a speed of 11.7 knots on a summer draught of 26.5 feet. But her trials soon revealed that when she steamed at over 10.58 knots she had greatly increased fuel consumption. In 1930 the ship was re-engined and fitted with a 6-cylinder Doxford, producing 3,435 bhp.

The introduction in 1925 of Isherwood's 'Bracketless' design of tanker construction, compounded with the subsequent centre tank, and two port and starboard wing tanks equalling centre-tank capacity, revolutionised the 1920s crude oil tanker. BP's *British Inventor*, built in 1926, was the first tanker to use Isherwood's revised patent, setting the basic design of the company's fleet for subsequent years. His modifications had arisen to compensate for the leakages that had occurred due to insufficient flexibility in the hull when the tanker was in any kind of seaway. Basically, to overcome this and other minor problems, he increased the strength of the longitudinal between bulkheads and adjacent transversals. He also eliminated his previous system of horizontal and vertical brackets surrounding the transversals separating individual cargo tanks, by fitting only two transversals, judicially placed within the tank. His resulting tanker soon found

The afterdeck of *British Aviator* showing the catwalk, by then a feature legally required to safeguard mariners travelling between the midships accommodation forward and aft. The tank tops are opened for airing purposes, and the valve and piping systems are clearly visible. *The Motor Ship*.

favour with Lloyd's Register, as it was easier to construct, reduced vibration and gave a modest saving in weight. Just as appealing to the ship owner, the vessel proved cheaper to operate. More importantly perhaps, Isherwood's modification helped tankers withstand more efficiently the enormous shearing forces experienced when some tanks were filled to 98 per cent capacity whilst others were empty.

The year 1930 saw important changes in the Load Line Convention, now permitting tankers of the newer class of 12,000 sdwt to load 15 inches below the previous summer draught load line. This not only increased efficiency and payload considerably, but gave equal parity to British tankers over their American-owned counterparts, which for many years had blatantly ignored the rules, operating with considerable advantage over the ships of the nations which had conformed.

Inevitably, increased capacity gradually followed in the BTC fleet. This led in 1936 to the launch of its *British Fame*, and created what would become its standard tanker, of around 12,000 sdwt capacity. She was the first of 12 similar tankers similar in every detail apart from the engines; this ship was propelled by a 4-cylinder William Doxford engine, as were five more ships, whereas the remaining six had Burmeister & Wain engines installed. The class were fitted with what had become traditional twin longitudinal bulkheads, and their nine transversals gave 30 oil tanks, with cargo discharged by four cargo pumps, each with capacity of 230 tons per hour. *British Fame* was built at Swan Hunter's yard and completed in October 1936. She carried her 12,250 sdwt on a draught of 27.7 feet at

British Inventor in 1926 was the first BTC tanker to benefit from the introduction of Isherwood's 'Bracketless' system of tank construction. A stronger ship resulted, which proved cheaper to build and gave a modest saving in weight, increasing the cargo-carrying capacity of the vessel and easier to maintain. Her keel was laid down originally in 1925 as British Ash, and she was launched the following year under the name in which she served the fleet. In 1940 British Inventor exploded a mine off St Alban's Head, and was eventually demolished in November of the same year. The Motor Ship.

a speed of 10 knots. Her gross tonnage was 8,303 tons. It is interesting to note how the respective gross tonnages of tankers around the 12,000 sdwt mark varied, for this vessel was some 400 tons lighter than others in this class. Possibly some minor differences in steel quality made a contribution towards this. The ship was 481 feet in length overall and 464.3 feet between perpendiculars, with a beam of 61.9 feet and moulded depth of 34 feet.

Using British Endurance as a representative vessel, the tanker was launched in August 1936, also from Swan Hunter's, and had the same dimensions as her sister ship. Similar to the remainder of the class, she was fitted with a cruiser stern that was gradually replacing the older counter stern, but retained the vertical stem. The ships were well equipped with four steel and two wooden lifeboats, each using the latest Wellin-MacLachlan gravity davits. Unique to BTC was the provision of additional staterooms giving their tankers a highly distinctive 'chunky' look amidships, which could not be mistaken for any other of the world's class of tankers.

As September 1939 approached, with overtones already gathered from crews who had served the previous conflict fresh in their minds, BTC's deep-sea and coastal fleet had its 100th tanker under construction, with its fleet totalling around one million tons capacity.

British Fame was launched in June 1936 at the Newcastle yards of Swan Hunter & Wigham Richardson and completed 14 months later. She served the company until 12 August 1940, when she was torpedoed whilst in Convoy OB193, between the UK and USA, by Italian submarine Malaspina. The Motor Ship.

The 1936 *British Endurance* was the second in this class of tankers. She came from the yards of Swan Hunter and had a deadweight tonnage on the summer load line of 12,250 tons. This tanker survived the ravages of the Second World War and served until January 1959 when she was sold to a Dutch company. Interestingly, it arranged for her to be rebuilt as a dry cargo ship and then, loaded with scrap metal, she sailed for Yawata in Japan, where she was demolished on arrival. *The Motor Ship.*

A group of inspectors from the international shipping magazine of some repute, *The Motor Ship*, were allowed to visit *British Endurance* and they were full of praise for this new class of tanker. They commented particularly favourably on the standard of accommodation for officers and ratings. Here are views they took on board of the officer's smoke room (equivalent to the wardroom on HM ships) and dining saloon, along with a shot of the captain's day room and a typical junior officer's cabin. *The Motor Ship*.

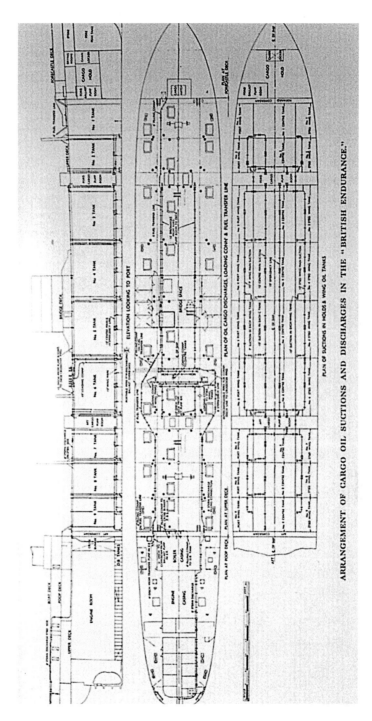

The cargo suctions and discharges diagram on the *British Endurance* was similar to that on all ships in this class. In the absence of a General Arrangement (GA) plan this shows the configuration of the cargo tanks and gives an idea of the main deck distribution of accommodation, derricks and tank tops. *The Motor Ship*.

TWO

The ravages of war: 1939–1945

The Second World War events affecting the Merchant Navy have been thoroughly documented and researched elsewhere. The involvement of the BTC proved no exception, for fundamentally it suffered drastic losses in crews and ships, alongside many other British merchant companies, especially those operating the tankers which all too soon became prime targets of enemy action.

The company's first tanker loss was, by a strange quirk of fate, the last ship launched before the conflict began. She was *British Influence*, typical of the class at 12,443 sdwt. She was completed from Swan Hunter's Newcastle yards in May 1939, and just four months later was torpedoed and sunk. A favourite spot for submarines to aim their torpedoes was of course the engine room and when the missile found its mark there were bound to be numerous casualties. I recall, when serving as a young navigating cadet, speaking to an engineering officer who had served in the conflict. His words were almost nonchalant: 'These things were rarely thought about: you just got on with the job, otherwise you'd go mad' – although, even to a naïve 16-year-old a certain look in his eyes spoke quietly of thoughts and feelings residing far more deeply than words could convey.

The last casualty was *British Freedom*. This ship had been completed in June 1928 at Palmer's Newcastle shipyards. At 10,440 sdwt and 7,066 grt she was 456.8 feet overall

Whilst on passage from Abadan to Hull in September 1939, *British Influence* was stopped by U-29 south-west of Eire, and became the first ship owned by BTC to be sunk in the Second World War. In those early days of 'wartime courtesy' the crew were permitted to abandon their ship, which was then sunk by gunfire and torpedo. Roly Weekes.

British Freedom was the last BTC tanker to be sunk. She was on passage under Admiralty charter from Halifax to the UK when shortly after leaving port on 14 January 1945, whilst on charter to the Admiralty, she was sunk by a torpedo from U-1232. The prominent wooden latticework structure above the midships wheelhouse is for the rigging of protective awnings from the sun in tropical waters. Roly Weekes.

and 440.1 feet between perpendiculars, with a beam of 57.1 feet and moulded depth of 33.9 feet. She was torpedoed by U-1232 off Halifax on 14 January 1945.

Throughout the early to mid-stages of the war, when a range of technical and shipbuilding measures helped ease tanker and warship shortages, the UK and its allies suffered desperately from an inadequate number of the aircraft carriers. They had proved invaluable in the protection of convoys, by intercepting enemy spotter aircraft and, as their facilities became more sophisticated, sinking prowling submarines. With an inevitable shortage of these highly specialised vessels to serve even a minimum of the need, it was soon realised that the comparatively unhindered foredeck of a tanker could be readily adapted to serve as a mini-flight deck. Whilst a slimmer centre accommodation block was transferred to the starboard side, the ship could still carry a 90 per cent cargo load.

Following initial experiments, which resulted in just one aircraft being launched and the pilot baling out in the sea to be (hopefully) rescued by the tanker's attendant or other craft, improvements were made enabling additional aircraft to be carried. These tankers continued sailing under the red ensign, with Merchant Navy officers and crew, but Royal Naval ratings were carried to support the pilots and planes. The resulting tankers were called Merchant Aircraft Carriers (MAC); initially the Ministry of War Transport (MOWT) had selected vessels under construction and commandeered those seemingly most suitable over a range of areas. BTC and Shell Tankers eventually contributed the bulk of tankers, and ran these vessels on behalf of the MOWT.

It was in 1943 that the keel was laid in Cammell Laird's Birkenhead shipyard of the 168,869 sdwt *British Caution* when she attracted the attention of MAC government inspectors. Consequently, she was requisitioned by the MOWT, which promptly renamed her *Empire MacColl*; she was completed in May of that year, with BTC appointed as manager. Certainly, the success of the subsequent venture was proved in the following

The BTC tanker *British Caution* was still under construction in Cammell Laird's Birkenhead yards when she was requisitioned by the MOWT, and she sailed in May 1943 as the Merchant Aircraft Carrier (MAC ship) *Empire MacColl*. She survived the war, having performed sterling duties, and after the conflict ended was purchased by BTC and renamed *British Pilot*. Roly Weekes.

British Pilot seen here in her peacetime BTC colours. The extent of the rebuilding necessary to convert her to normal tanker trading is evident when comparison is made with the previous photograph. The tanker served the company well, and was eventually broken up at Faslane in August 1962. Roly Weekes.

Fuelling naval warships at sea was conducted initially by a fuel pipe to the warship, fed from a stem-fitted boom on the tanker. *British Vigour*, launched in 1942, was one such merchant vessel adapted. This 8,485 sdwt, 406.2-foot tanker was completed in the yards of Furness Shipbuilding at Haverton Hill, Stockton-on-Tees, in February 1943. *The Motor Ship*.

Seen in her peacetime colours, *British Vigour* was converted, following the conflict, to peacetime trading. She served BTC until sold to French owner, the Compagnie d'Armement Maritime, in 1959 and renamed *Thoronet*. It was under this name that she was eventually scrapped at Avilés, northern Spain, in June 1964. G. Brownell.

voyages for in the two remaining years of the war few of the over 200 convoys escorted by MAC ships experienced serious submarine assault, and a number of U-boats were sunk.

A further operation in which the Merchant Navy helped its Royal Naval cousins was replenishment of the fleet with fuel oil whilst on passage. It was initially a delicate problem, in that the escorting warships had to leave their convoys, often at a crucial period, in order to proceed into the nearest oil port for bunkering. Early experiments showed, however, that merchant naval tankers could be adapted to carry fuel oils, and often lighter oils, and then – initially by means of a boom fitted over the stem of the tanker – the fuel lines could be easily retrieved by Allied warships. It was not much later into the war that derricks and booms were fitted to tankers, enabling up to two warships

A BTC ship in full grey-painted wartime regalia. The 12,202 sdwt *British Might* was completed from the yards of Blythewood Shipbuilding in Glasgow on 20 July 1935. She was fully armed with five guns: two aft, two on the bridge wings and one for'ard. Additional to her regular complement of lifeboats, there were four life-rafts that could be either launched or released manually. These subsequently saved many lives when severe damage and fire prevented the lifeboats from being launched; for navies of all nations involved in the conflict, tankers with their distinctive outline soon became prime targets. *British Might* survived the war and continued in company service until she was scrapped at Troon, on the Ayrshire coast, in May 1961. BP Plc.

to come alongside and fuel simultaneously off the port and starboard beams without reducing speed: a great asset. BTC joined Shell Tankers as leaders in this field, and a number of tankers from each company were subsequently used.

Apart from specialised MAC and RAS conversions, BTC continued a modest but quite consistent programme of tanker shipbuilding throughout the war; in fact the only years in which no ships were delivered were 1940 and 1944. The company directors were never tempted to order any of the mass-produced hence prolific T2 class of American-built tankers, but continued to order their vessels built from what had become traditional British yards. This trend continued after the war ended, although they then chartered a number of the mass-produced tankers.

Four BTC vessels were actively involved in D-Day, and although *British Engineer* was damaged by a mine all the BTC ships survived this epic landing. Little has been said in this book about the company's small but diverse coastal fleet, but *British Scout* was actively involved in D-Day by transporting parcels of assorted fuel oils to the Mulberry harbour at Arromanches. This 2,210 sdwt tanker had been completed by Harland and Wolff in October 1922. She was 1,507 grt, with an overall length of 245 feet, a 37.2 feet moulded beam and a depth of 19.8 feet. Her 3-cylinder 910 bhp engine was manufactured by the builders and gave a varying speed of around 8 knots. The ship served until April 1957, when she went for demolition by Metal Industries Limited at Rosyth.

Harland and Wolff's Glasgow yards completed *British Merit* in July 1942 along with her 6-cylinder 2,450 bhp engine. The tanker was 11,961 sdwt, with an overall length of 463.2 feet, a 61.2-foot beam and 33.1 feet moulded depth. The vessel survived the war but became a casualty when on 25 July 1942 (whilst still on her maiden voyage) she was torpedoed by U-552 whilst sailing in Convoy ON113 between the UK and Newfoundland, 600 miles east of her destination. She was taken in tow to Newfoundland and eventually repaired in New York later the same year. The vessel was demolished at Briton Ferry in April 1961. G. Brownell.

British Virtue was another tanker completed for BTC in June 1945 from the yards of Swan Hunter. With a sdwt of 12,390 and an overall length of 469 feet, she was very much a standard tanker for the company at this time. She survived the war, remaining in service with BTC until she was scrapped at Troon in May 1962. Skyfotos.

One of the few coastal tankers which over the years were built by various British yards for BTC. *British Scout* was launched by Harland and Wolff's Newcastle yards on 25 August 1922. This 2,210 sdwt ship performed sterling service by transporting assorted fuel oils to the Mulberry harbour during D-Day and remained with the Company until she was scrapped at Rosyth in 1957. World Ship Society.

THREE

Recovery: 1946–1950, a time of optimism

The condition of the BTC fleet immediately after the war was not very healthy; 44 company-owned tankers had been sunk, along with a further 6 managed ships, but in 1945 the fleet still numbered 69 tankers. Regarding the company's seagoing staff, the cost was truly horrific, with 675 killed and many physically injured, whilst psychological scars were carried to the grave by most of the surviving crew members. The men were war-weary, whilst most of the ships stood tired and in urgent need of adequate repairs. The necessity of putting tankers to work as quickly as possible to meet the inevitable requirements, meant that dry dockings and surveys had been rushed, with very often only essential repairs being effected in order to meet the requirements of the next Certificate of Seaworthiness, rather than anything more beneficial.

The termination of hostilities engendered an ethos of revaluation. And there was much to revalue. Not only were answers required to the questions of how to rejuvenate the fleet, but many refineries had been damaged during the war, leaving them in urgent need of repair.

British Success was completed in February 1946, having been launched from the yards of Blythewood Shipbuilding on 7 November 1945. Due to draft restrictions imposed by navigating the Suez Canal, she continued the successful 1930s class of 12,000 sdwt tankers with similar dimensions, including a draft of 27.6 feet adequate to meet demands of the canal at 29 feet. The tanker continued in service until September 1957 when she was laid up in Falmouth, and was eventually towed to Troon in 1961. In October of that year she was broken up. G. Brownell.

Right – This montage of photographs shows the GA plan of *British Marquis*, indicating that although the tank configuration and internal structural arrangements remain largely unaltered, subtle changes have developed in the hull form, with a move away from the straight stem to one that was more slightly curved, and a more slightly raked cruiser stern. The GA plan shows the lowered radar mast, suggesting that masts also were telescopic, enabling transits to be made to the tanker jetties at Stanlow on the Manchester Ship Canal. Photo 3.2 shows gas risers just visible on the fore and main masts. These assist pressure in the cargo tanks to equalise as the ship sails between different temperature zones whilst on passage between loading and discharge ports. The apparently unusual number of halyards, and the triatic stay between foremast and after accommodation, assisted the hoisting of flags and other legal signals, including Not Under Command shapes and lights. Canvas wind funnels were also supported; these were inserted into the cargo tanks before tank cleaning to assist with gas dispersal, and afterwards to help airing and drying of tanks prior to the pre-loading inspection before receiving a new cargo. A further external change is the removal of the crow's nest on the foremast, so much a feature of earlier vessels. In both photos the ships are flying international code flags above the wheelhouse block: letter H, *pilot on board*, and the red B burgee – essential for all tankers – *the ship carries a dangerous cargo, or is in a potentially explosive condition*. The carriage of two lifeboats, in more modern davits, on each accommodation block was a legal requirement, with originals dating back to 1912 following safety recommendations made after the inquiries into the *Titanic* disaster. Aboard tankers, each block had to carry sufficient boats to convey the crew to safety regardless of a list of the ship, and in instances when an outbreak of fire isolated crews in one or another area of the ship. By now all ratings were regularly housed aft, with deck officers and 'sparks' midships on the upper bridge deck, and all engineering officers, including the chief, on the bridge deck below. The high indication of both ships show that each is in ballast. Later tankers were fitted with stern loading and discharging pipes helping cater for the new oil fields increasingly being opened that had restricted jetty access. One such port was Falconara, on Italy's Adriatic coast, which received crude oil and exported a range of products. Ancona Bay, serving this port, had been dredged shortly beforehand, to receive tankers drawing up to 18 feet. GA plan, *The Motor Ship*. Photo, World Ship Society.

Yet for all that, across a range of areas within most of the world there had existed since 1945 an increased and ever-increasing demand for oil. The post-war customers of BP, as the parent company, came – perhaps surprisingly – from other oil companies and associated third parties buying crude oil, together with increasing markets opening for fuel oil transported by BP's shipping arm, BTC. This was the period when, for instance, industry and power stations ashore were converting from coal to oil at an unprecedented rate – and additionally, and perhaps equally unexpectedly - private car ownership was expanding rapidly worldwide, bringing its own seemingly unquenchable demands for oil products.

In the UK the sense of relief translated itself into a determination for improvement, which to BTC meant designing a modern type of tanker. Foremost in the thoughts of the directors was to increase tonnage capacity of their ships, but they had always been mindful to build tankers that could meet draft restrictions in that vitally important seaway, the Suez Canal. Their versatile 12,000 sdwt class tankers, for example, had a summer draft of around 27 feet 10 inches, which was adequate to meet the dredged channel depth of 29 feet, although increasing clamours for a deeper waterway implied that inevitably it would not be too long before modest dredging operations would deepen the main channel. In 1947 BP bought ten T2 tankers averaging 16,500 sdwt with an overall length of 506 feet, beam 68 feet and moulded depth around 39 feet. Although

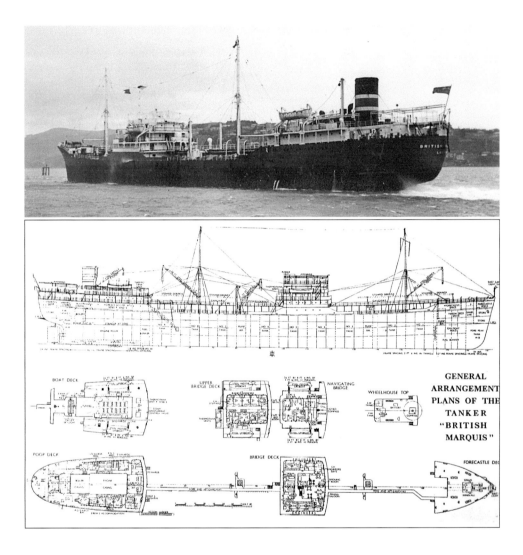

GENERAL ARRANGEMENT PLANS OF THE TANKER "BRITISH MARQUIS"

useful for the world's markets, the draft of these versatile ships, at just over 30 feet, exceeded 29 feet implying limitations in their use of the Suez Canal. Whilst the T2s more than justified their investment, these sturdy tankers, originally built for just one Atlantic crossing, drank so much fuel as they grew older that they became uneconomic. With an eye to an optimistic future, an ambitious programme of new building was implemented, commencing with 57 tankers ordered from British shipyards.

The company's first post-war tanker was the 12,490 sdwt *British Success*. The ship was one in a list of ships coming from the yards of the Blythewood Shipbuilding Company and, launched in November 1945, beat her sister ship *British Caution* by some two months, although both were completed in February 1946. She served until September 1957 when she was laid up in Falmouth, and was eventually scrapped at Troon on 20 October 1961.

The fourth tanker in this ambitious programme of remodelling the fleet was British Marquis. Completed on 1 June 1946 at William Doxford's Sunderland yards at 12,310 sdwt and, with her 4-cylinder oil engine producing 3,435 bhp, the ship had a service speed around 12 knots. Once again, the supportive magazine The Motor Ship was invited to send representatives to inspect this new unit, and the following series of photographs illustrates admirably ideas emanating from new thinking behind BTC's 'modern' tanker.

Whilst The Motor Ship's reporters were on board, they were permitted to take a number of internal photographs covering engine room, officer and crew accommodation and facilities, and on the bridge.

Many of the steering gears fitted to British Marquis and other tankers in the class were manufactured by Clarke Chapman Marine of Gateshead. The company also innovated and provided a wide range of modern deck gear including windlasses and winches. The steering gear was either of the two- or four-ram type which, to conform to Classification Society regulations, had to be capable of turning the helm from hard-a-port to hard-a-starboard over 30 degrees on either side, in 30 seconds. Although the gear was operated hydraulically, it had to be capable of manual turning. Which type of ram was fitted was determined by technical specifications derived by comparing the rudder area with the square of the ship's speed. The Motor Ship.

The wheelhouse of the *British Marquis* showing the modern steering gear, engine room telegraph, gyrocompass and depth sounder on the bulkhead above the flag locker. *The Motor Ship.*

British Marquis' cargo control room was modern and comprehensive, complementing a range of deck valves. From this office, the entire operation could be carried out: controlling the cargo flow whilst loading and discharging and also during ballasting operations. Outside the picture would be a mimic board (as it would later be known) showing the relative positions of every cargo and ballast valve aboard the ship. All valves were numbered for reference. Cargo and separate ballast pumps could be controlled from here; they were fitted with glass panels indicating the state of each. *The Motor Ship.*

Completed on 25 November, *British Captain* was the last of 27 tankers delivered in 1948 and 1949. Within a few days she had embarked upon her maiden voyage. The ship, at 12,303 sdwt, came from Harland and Wolff's Glasgow yards. She was one of a number of BTC ships powered by a 3,480 bhp 6-cylinder diesel engine manufactured by the builders. The tanker continued in service until 4 December 1962 when she arrived at Faslane and work commenced on her demolition. Roly Weekes.

FOUR

Emergence – growth in the 1950s

Upheavals of international politics in the 1950s rarely remained far below the surface of the turbulent waters associated with any ship engaged on operations in the Middle East. This became built on the tensions already created in 1948 by the first Arab-Israeli conflict, when Haifa oil terminal suddenly found itself devoid of oil from the Gulf. Certainly, the fortunes of British Petroleum, parent company to its shipping arm, BTC, were irrevocably affected by burning unrest in this region.

In the year 1951 erupted the first of a number of boiling points. This particular *fracas* began, apparently innocently enough, with a number of unreasonable demands introduced by a new government in Iran. As these could not be immediately resolved, the Iranian government nationalised Anglo-Iranian Oil's considerably substantial investments in the Persian Gulf. The dispute led BP to cease trading to the port of Abadan later in the year, enabling negotiations to be re-established later on a more amicable footing. The immediate effect proved equally irrevocable, however. All company operations ceased in that port, resulting in a worldwide shortage of oil. The Gulf was not completely closed to BP, however, for Kuwait retained its historical loyalty towards Britain, enabling the port of Mina Al Ahmadi not only to remain open but able to take the opportunity to expand – as indeed did Bahrain.

Exercising the same kind of *prescience* which had benefited Anglo-Iranian oil since its conception by William Knox D'Arcy when he had founded the parent company, Anglo-Persian Oil, in 1909, the current board of directors had perhaps seen something of 'the writing on the wall'. The company was already constructing terminals outside this tension-filled region to help cope with increasing market demands for oil, as well as potentially anticipating more political unrest in the Gulf. In the UK, for example, harbour developments were under construction at the Isle of Grain in Kent, at Grangemouth, at Finnart on the banks of Loch Long, and at Llandarcy at Swansea in south Wales. On the Continent, new oil ports were being built at Lavera (in the south of France), Dunkirk, Hamburg and Antwerp. A new pipeline had been constructed across Scotland, connecting the new refinery at Finnart with the port of Grangemouth.

As early as September 1949 (doubtless with the ramifications in mind of the experiences of Haifa), BP Limited ordered for BTC a series of two larger 16,000 sdwt

In a move away from BTC's 1,200 sdwt class, *British Freedom* was the first BTC tanker of increased capacity. She was completed by Swan Hunter's in February 1950 at 16,849 sdwt with a length overall of 525.5 feet. Her 6-cylinder engine was designed by Wallsend Slipway Company and on the test bed developed 6,400 bhp, giving a service speed around 14 knots on her summer draft marks. She was demolished at Kaohsiung in April 1972. G. Brownell.

Another view of *British Freedom*, showing that although she was of slightly increased capacity, this is not particularly noticeable on viewing the ship, apart from an increase in overall length: 525.5 feet as against 469.6, beam 69.8 feet as against 61.9, and moulded depth 37.5 feet as against 33.6. In keeping with all tankers around this tonnage, the length to depth ratio was invariably built around 12.5:1. Skyfotos.

tankers, together with two of the standard handy size 12,000 sdwt, along with a number of ships of smaller capacity.

On 30 March 1949, *British Freedom*, the first of the increased capacity ships, was launched from the yards of Swan Hunter, whilst the second, *British Response*, followed on 23 September 1949 from James Laing's yards in nearby Sunderland. *Freedom* was the first to be completed, in February 1950, preceding her sister, *Response*, by some four months. *Freedom* carried forward a company tradition of passing down the same names to subsequent new buildings, for she was the second tanker to bear this name. (The first, at 10,440 sdwt, had been built in 1928 by Palmer's of Newcastle, and on passage between Halifax and the UK had become a casualty of a torpedo from U-1232.) The new tanker was 16,849 sdwt, 11,207 grt, with an overall length of 525.5 feet, beam 69.8 feet and depth 37.5 feet. She was powered by a 6-cylinder Doxford oil engine manufactured by Wallsend Slipway Company, generating 6,400 bhp. Although BTC continued ordering its 12,000 sdwt tonnage tankers, these two larger-capacity ships set patterns of thought that encouraged tanker designs with a more ambitious tonnage.

12 December 1950 saw further boardroom musings resulting in a further 19 tankers of various tonnages being accepted into the BTC fleet in 1951. Also that year, encouraged by the success of *British Freedom*, came the launching of *British Adventure* as the first in a class of tankers exceeding 30,000 sdwt. She was completed in September 1951 at Vickers Armstrong's Barrow-in Furness yards. With a summer deadweight capacity of 30,218 tons *British Adventure*'s length overall was 619.5 feet on a beam of 81.3 feet and depth 44.7 feet. She had nearly double the capacity of any of the company's tonnage to date, and at the time of her launching she was the largest tanker in the world. She was also the first of the company's tankers fitted with two steam turbine double-reduction engines, manufactured by Vickers, developing 13,750 shp, geared to a single propeller. This gave a laden service speed of 15 knots, making her the fastest ship owned by BTC. (The term 'shp' is applied to the power generated that drives the shaft on board the ship, rather than 'bhp', which refers to the power generated on the test bed ashore.) Just one month later *British Bulldog* was completed as the second in this class. It was from this time that the word 'supertanker' started being bandied around as a familiar term, doubtless aided by the popular press and their love of superfluities.

~~~~~~~~

BTC's 30,000-sdwt class of tanker gradually increased its fleet capacity throughout the 1950s. By 1951 the total fleet numbered 150 ships, with a similar number of chartered vessels. 1953 saw the completion of *British Sailor*, the first of the 14 tankers in this class ordered between 1952 and 1958. This 33,682 sdwt, 20,961 grt ship came from the Clydebank yards of John Brown & Company. She was 664 feet length overall and 640.6 feet between perpendiculars, with a beam of 86.7 feet and depth of 47 feet. Her engines

British Adventure was launched by Vickers Armstrong at its Barrow-in-Furness yards on 12 December 1950 and completed for BTC the following June. At 30,218 sdwt, 619.5 feet length overall, she was the largest tanker in the fleet. Her two steam turbine double-reduction engines geared to a single propeller shaft (also made by Vickers) developed 13,750 shp, giving her a service speed of 15 knots, making her its fastest vessel at the time. She served the company until 1973, when she was sold to Greek interests and renamed *Vrahos*. They ran her until 1975, when she was scrapped in Kaohsiung. BP Plc.

This impressive shot shows the launching of *British Bulldog* from the Wallsend yards of Swan Hunter on 22 May 1951. This 30,099 sdwt, 619.5-foot overall length tanker was the second in the class of nine ships delivered from various British yards to BTC. She was finally demolished on 12 July 1972 by Spanish shipbreakers in the port of Castellon, just north of Valencia. *Tanker Times* magazine.

The year 1951 alone saw 19 tankers of various tonnages accepted into the BTC fleet, whilst the number of ships it owned exceeded 150, with the many chartered vessels. Certainly, markets were readily found for the new class of 30,000 sdwt ships, but the 'standard' 12,000 tonners continued to be built, as well, together with a class of smaller vessels that served the ever-growing products markets. One of these latter tankers was *British Lady*, a handy size vessel of 8,463 sdwt, 6,140 grt, with an overall length of 406.7 feet, completed by Smiths Dry Dock Company of Middlesbrough in June of that year. She was powered by a 3-cylinder oil engine, manufactured by Hawthorn, Leslie's of Newcastle, that was capable of developing 2,250 bhp. The ship served the company until August 1963 when she was scrapped at Bowness. Roly Weekes.

were manufactured by the builders and they, similar to other vessels in this larger class, were two double-reduction steam turbines,geared to a single propeller. They developed 13,750 shp (12,500 bhp), giving a service speed of nearly 15 knots on a summer draft of 35 feet. She was fitted with the stern discharge pipe that had become a standard fitting for many BTC ships as they began calling at ports recently created resulting from increasing international demands for oil arising to a lesser extent from tensions in the Middle East. With the influx into the fleet of larger tankers, a clearer defined demarcation emerged, with this class becoming increasingly used for crude and dirty oils, and the smaller tonnages transporting a range of products.

Following extensive negotiations, 1954 saw the reopening of relationships with the oil-producing company in Iran, resulting in Abadan again becoming operational. As a delicate part of the talks, it was decided that from December of that year the parent Anglo-Iranian Oil Company Limited should change its name to British Petroleum Company Limited. It was from October 1954 that a shield was added to the familiar BP funnel on board the company tankers, with *British Soldier* becoming the first ship to carry this adornment. Simultaneously that kingdom of oil wells, called the Persian Gulf, which had become almost a household name to tanker types, tactfully changed its name to the Arabian Gulf.

Dressed overall and with her pilot on board, *British Sailor* is seen on passage heading for her first port of discharge. This 33,682 sdwt tanker was launched at the Clydeside yards of John Brown in December 1952 and completed just four months later. She was 664 feet in length (oa) and her twin steam turbines gave her a service speed of nearly 15 knots on a summer draft of 47 feet. The tanker served the company until 1972, when she was sold to Cyprian interests who renamed her *Marisira*. The Cypriot owner ran her for two years, then an Egyptian ship owner bought her and renamed her *Fagr*. In 1980, after nearly 30 years of service, she was demolished at Kaohsiung. BP Plc.

The GA plan of *British Sailor* shows the displacement of cargo tanks and details of officer/crew accommodation, making an interesting comparison with *British Marquis* (1946 – Photo 3.2.) The after boat deck offered two additional staterooms supplementing the two midships on the navigating bridge deck. Petty officers were quartered on the poop deck, with deck and engine room ratings along the starboard and port sides respectively on the upper deck. The petty officers had a separate mess deck aft of the officer's dining room and smoke room.

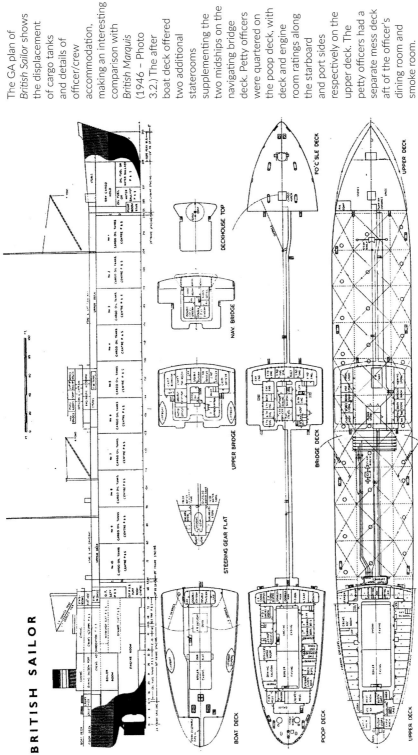

BRITISH SAILOR

BTC offered deck and engineering officers and ratings a solid career structure, and this, combined with equally solid standards of catering and accommodation for all crews, gave the company considerable credibility with seafarers. In the 1950s–1970s BTC was recognised as 'a good firm with whom to build a career'. Certainly, the officer's smoke room and crew recreation room on *British Sailor* epitomised the advantages gained from the extra space available in such large-capacity tankers. The improvements in décor and comfort of the officers' smoke room aboard this tanker compare favourably with that of the *British Endurance* (1936 – Photo 1.7.) The 1950s represented a peak period for the British Merchant Navy, which was undoubtedly (and stated as proven fact) the largest and best in the world, with many companies competing for personnel. Both shots *Tanker Times* magazine.

British Advocate held the distinction in 1954 of being the first BP tanker to celebrate the resumption of the company's trading in the port of Abadan. The ship was completed in July 1948 at Lithgow's Port Glasgow yard, and was one of the company's 12,300 sdwt capacity ships. She was scrapped in 1962 at Bilbao in Spain. G. Brownell.

The 16,870 sdwt *British Vision* under way in ballast was completed in July 1954 at the yards of Thompson and Sons, Sunderland. This new class in tankers of the same capacity varies slightly with the earlier batch that was launched with *British Chivalry* in 1949, until 1951. These were all of 525.5 feet length (bp), 69.8 feet beam and 37.5 feet depth. Those completed just a few years later were 547 feet (bp), and the same 69.8 feet beam, but of just 30 feet moulded depth, giving a tanker whose additional length and reduced depth facilitated transits of the Suez Canal until it could be re-dredged. *British Vision* remained with BP until 1972 when she was scrapped in Spain. Roly Weekes.

The foredeck of *British Vision* showing modern rounded tank tops, main cargo lines and deck valves. The safety function of the legal requirement catwalk is clearly demonstrated; for certainly, negotiating this cluttered working area with the ship fully laden, in anything but the calmest weather, could prove extremely dangerous. *The Motor Ship.*

1955 was a quiet year for British Petroleum, seeing the launch of only one tanker, the 32,000 sdwt *British Victory*. But the state of the fleet, a mere ten years after boardroom reviews into that aspect of the company's future, clearly indicated the acumen not only of its planning but the determination to 'make it happen' (to use a later but appropriate company term). Of its 138 ships in service during 1936 there were: 12 tankers in the 32,000 sdwt class; 6 of 28,000, 20 of 16,000, and 80 of the 12,000 sdwt which had replaced the 'handy sized' 10,000 tonners (of which just 3 remained). This class of ships was used on different voyages to carry both crude oil and products, but with the advent of the tankers of increased capacity they were then used purely for crude oil cargoes. The remainder were tankers operating below 8,000 sdwt. Additionally, two coasters were jointly owned with Shell-Mex Company. With orders placed for 32 ships in various stages of construction distributed around the company's traditional major British shipbuilding yards, the new buildings would give the BP fleet a total of 170 tankers.

Developments in design of *British Vision* across a range of areas with earlier tankers makes interesting comparisons with Photo 1.3, of the 1924 *British Aviator* class of tanker, shows improvements in technology facilitating cargo handling and spaciousness. For crew comfort, a swimming pool was placed aft on the port side of the funnel. *The Motor Ship*.

1956 saw no new ships launched, but it did produce an international crisis built around ownership of the Suez Canal and the nationalisation of this by one Gamal Abdel Nasser. The 103 miles of the canal had remained a vital link since its opening in 1869, and it was in 1914 that its channel had been dredged to 29 feet. Through 1957 this important waterway remained closed, hitting the world's ship operators hard, especially as 60 per cent of Europe's oil had until then been carried through Suez. BP certainly felt the impact: while a return trip from Coryton, on the Thames Estuary, to the Gulf via Suez is approximately 13,000 nautical miles, around Cape Agulhas it is 22,000 miles.

Virtually double the steaming distance meant considerably increased bunkering costs, but there was more bad news: a 10 per cent cut in the consumption of oil was imposed in Britain, which inevitably resulted in a shortage not only at the pumps, affecting all car owners, but in the wider transportation system of road, rail and aircraft.

Within the company, the closure fired an unexpected measure of boardroom replanning that would be built around its transport arm. The British Tanker Company

Limited (BTC) had two years earlier been restyled as BP Tanker Company Limited, but now a number of future company transfers and mergers was planned. Thoughts about the best methods of financing these led to a range of boardroom machinations.

Foremost in the minds of its directors was yet another possible future canal closure and how this might be confronted. The question basically had to be built around questions of costs involved regarding transportation. For, to use practical figures, the 16,000 sdwt tanker could (theoretically, depending largely on the specific gravity and temperature of the oil) carry 4.2 million gallons of crude, whilst a 30,000 sdwt ship could potentially carry 8.4 million gallons. Both vessels could well become the new 'handy sized' vessel capable of carrying both clean and dirty cargoes, yet providing sufficiently versatility to enter most of the new ports that, governed by customer needs, continued to spring up around the world.

The board acted quickly, and 1957 saw the first of its suddenly planned moves. In January Tanker Transport Company came into being to finance a new fleet rebuilding project. This, underwritten by two financiers, A.C. Lenton and Robert Fleming, formed Ship Mortgages Limited. Tankers would be leased to BP with an option to purchase after 22 years' service. The same year saw completion of two 16,000-tonners; the launching of one tanker at 33,702 sdwt, and two ships each with a capacity of 35,572 sdwt. Common Brothers of Newcastle became the manager of three 1936/7 tankers, *British Confidence*, *British Fortitude* and *British Diligence*, that were renamed with the prefix *Anglian*.

British Diligence was launched by Swan Hunter's in December 1936. She was one of the standard 12,235 sdwt class of tankers that survived the war to serve BTC and BP Tanker Company. In 1957 Common Brothers of Newcastle took over her management and renamed her *Anglian Diligence*. Under this name the tanker continued service until 1958, when she was scrapped at Genoa. Skyfotos.

October 1957 saw the completion of the first 35,256 sdwt tanker, *British Valour*, by Swan Hunter. The ship was 680 feet (loa) and 640 feet (bp), with a beam of 86.5 feet. She was the first of two high-speed tankers, and her 22,500 shp steam turbine engines, aided by a bulbous bow, gave her a service speed of around 17.5 knots on summer draught of 35.1 feet. This is a remarkable service speed for any tanker, and has rarely been exceeded even by the larger tonnage eventually to reach the oil markets, the average charter speed for VLCCs, for example, ranging around (an often optimistic) 16–16.5 knots. The hull – largely welded, with rivets in the bilge turn construction, sheer strake and gunwale bar – was particularly strong. In 1973 she was transferred under her existing name to Tanker Charter Company, and remained in service until October 1972 when she was demolished at Castellon. Here she is seen entering port with a statutory tug in attendance. Roly Weekes.

The last ship to be completed in 1958 was in December of that year, the *British Ambassador*. This 44,929 sdwt, 710 foot long, 95.3 foot beam tanker was completed by Vickers Armstrong's Barrow-in-Furness yards for the BP Tanker Company, and at that time was the largest vessel in its fleet. In 1975, whilst on passage between Ras Tanura, in the Gulf, and Los Angeles, and 180 miles west of Iwo Jima her engine room flooded. This proved impossible to control and she had to be abandoned, fortunately without loss of life. Roly Weekes.

Impressive views of the launching on 2 June 1958, and sea trials in October of that year, of *British Duchess*, delivered from the yards of John Brown, Glasgow. This tanker was the second of a class of 44,000 ships delivered to BP Tanker Company. She was transferred immediately to Tanker Charter Company but reverted to BP Tanker Company in 1972. The vessel served until 1975 when she was sold to Greek interests, with J. Latsis, a reputable London-Greek manager, operating the ship. She was renamed *Petrola XXV*, then in 1976 was renamed *Petrola 25*. It was under this final name that she was demolished at Barcelona in 1978. Both photographs BP Plc.

Twelve tankers of varying tonnages were accepted in 1958 by BP Tanker Company as either transfers or new deliveries. Following company policy, there was a gradual increase in tonnage capacity of the latter from 33,454 sdwt to the 44,929-ton *British Ambassador*. (She was the second tanker to carry this name, her predecessor an 11,000 sdwt ship built at the Sunderland yards of J. Laing in 1924.) She survived the war and served the company until July 1954 when she was scrapped at Bowness.

The years 1956 to 1958 were turbulent times for the tanker industry, and in some respects for the shipping industry generally. Inevitably this affected BP Tanker Company. Continuing the boardroom policy of providing funds to extend the fleet renewal, British Petroleum Company Limited responded by creating Clyde Charter Company, under whose umbrella a number of new buildings were ordered and transferred. Further negotiations with a Danish ship-owning company and the British ship owner, Houlder Brothers resulted in the founding of Nordic Tankships A/S and Warwick Tankers Limited. The company by now was spreading its ownership/management net pretty widely to include names of shipping companies not normally associated with tanker management.

In 1959 Denholm of Glasgow on behalf of Clyde Charter Company undertook the management of the three 1937-built tankers, *British Integrity, British Fidelity* and *British Destiny,* renaming them with the prefix *Gaelic.*

BP Tanker Company continued the policy of gradually increasing the capacity of its ships, with an order already placed for a vessel of around 65,000 sdwt. Meanwhile, on 16 September 1959 a landmark launching, by Her Majesty Queen Elizabeth the Queen Mother, was the 49,967 sdwt *British Queen* from the Clydebank yards of John Brown and Company. In December of that year the ship was transferred to Tanker Charter Company. She had originally been planned for a capacity of 42,000 sdwt, but later instructions agreed enlargement to just under 50,000 sdwt. She was the first of the 12 large tankers ordered as a result of the strategy to operate tankers with an ever-increasing capacity range exceeding 60,000 sdwt.

Bearing in mind the importance of enhanced technical details regarding this larger tonnage, it is worth spreading a few words on tanker specifications. For a start *British Queen* was the largest ship ever launched on the Clyde since the *Queen Mary* some 21 years earlier. *British Queen* had an overall length of 760 feet and was designed for outward voyages from European ports through Suez, with a return passage via the Cape, owing to the canal's capacity restrictions to around 42,000 tons. Her accommodation was to the highest order: air-conditioned cabins and working spaces were provided, along with single cabins for all crew except apprentices or cadets and deck/catering boys. Geared steam turbine engines developed 16,000 shp, giving a service speed of 15.5 knots on a summer draught of 40.5 feet. The propeller was five-bladed with a diameter of 21 feet, and weighed 25 tons. Her cargo space was traditional, but with three longitudinal oil-tight bulkheads and ten transversals, giving her 44 tanks, with three of the wing tanks port

In January 1937 Harland and Wolff's Glasgow yard completed the 12,176 sdwt *British Destiny* (later, *British Destiny 1*). This ship was one of six tankers managed under a company reorganisation plan implemented in 1957. Denholm of Glasgow undertook responsibility for her management, and she was renamed *Gaelic Destiny*. She was scrapped at Rotterdam in 1959. World Ship Society.

and starboard designed for permanent ballast. This seawater capacity was additional, of course, to that carried by all tankers by this time in the fore and aft peak tanks. The three cargo pumps had a capacity of 1,250 tons per hour, whilst the water ballast pump had a capacity of 750 tons/hour, with the two cargo stripping pumps each operating at 250 tons/hour. The single ballast stripping pump operated at 150 tons/hour. Theoretically, loading could occur in 13 hours (using shore pumps) and discharge in around 15 hours, but in reality this optimum figure was rarely attained, largely due to unforeseen difficulties that occur (almost inevitably) to bedevil all tanker operations. The kind of things which might occur are problems arising from faulty valves which stick unexpectedly; human error affecting the staggering pattern in loading/discharging cargoes, creating delays, or the development of a sudden fault arising in any kind of equipment.

British Queen was fitted with a total of 13 tons of magnesium anodes, with her ballast tanks coated as protection against corrosion. The 16-inch radar display was fitted with the latest reflection plotter, enabling international regulation collision-avoidance triangles to be completed using chinagraph pencils, to offer at least an indication of any specific target's movements.

April 1959 saw another unique event, but one perhaps more reflective of the internal political ramifications affecting British shipbuilding and the unions rather than arising

These two views of BP Tanker Company's *British Queen* show the impressive lines of this ship. She was built by John Brown's Clydebank shipyards, completed in December 1959 and immediately transferred to Tanker Charter Company Limited, London. At 49,967 sdwt the ship was of 32,414 grt with an overall length of 760 feet, 725 feet (bp), beam of 97 feet, and a moulded depth of 54 feet. She was powered by a double-reduction geared steam turbine constructed by the builders to Pametrada (Parsons and Marine Engineering Turbine Research and Development Association) design, developing 16,000 shp and giving her a service speed of 15.5 knots on a summer draught of 40.5 feet. The ship was transferred back to BP Tanker Company in 1972 and was eventually scrapped at Kaohsiung on 16 June 1975. BP Plc and World Ship Society.

British Destiny 2 was a 44,902 sdwt tanker completed at the yards of Swan Hunter in December 1959 for BP Tanker Company, and transferred across to Clyde Charter Company later the same month. The chartroom aft of, yet part of, the wheelhouse area, shows the typically modern facilities that were so much a feature of the 'new streamlined Company image', yet many of the essentially familiar instruments, so comforting to new navigators joining the vessel, were retained. This tanker was transferred back to the parent company in 1972 and just three years later, on being sold to Liberian interests, was renamed *Agia Trias*. She remained with the company until 1979, when she entered the fleet of the Singapore-registered company Nai Tio Ocean Transport, which afforded her the delightful name *Rallytime* I. It was under this name that she was scrapped on Gadani Beach, Pakistan, in December 1982. Roly Weekes and *Tanker Times* magazine.

from international affairs – both of those, though, equally outside the remit of this book. The event resulted in BP Tanker Company taking delivery of its first ship from a foreign yard. The tanker was *British Light*, and she was the first in a series of six ships ordered from Ansaldo SpA Genoa and Cantieri Riuniti dell' Adriatico of Trieste.

In 1959 Italian yards produced a total of 11 deep-sea tankers for various international ship owners. Constructed at Ansaldo's, *British Light* was 36,754 sdwt with an overall length of 683 feet and beam 86.3 feet. Her by now almost conventional double-geared steam turbine engines developed 14,000 shp at a fast service speed of around 17 knots on a summer draught of 37.7 feet. Her ten main cargo tanks were subdivided by the traditional two longitudinal bulkheads resulting in a total of 30 tanks. It would appear that the ship experienced electrical problems that seemed unresolvable for much of her career, leading to yet another of the endless frustrations often bedevilling officers taking their ships away to sea. Notwithstanding these problems the tanker served the fleet until 1975.

The tanker *British Light* was the first ship owned by the BP Tanker Company to be built abroad. She was launched in the Genoa yards of Ansaldo SpA on 10 October 1958 at 36,754 sdwt, and completed the following April. Among modern features of this ship was the unusual stem which followed the usual rake until reaching almost to the boot topping at the loaded waterline, when it descended vertically. This feature is just visible in the photograph. The vessel was finally laid up for four months in London until she arrived at Bilbao for scrapping on 27 May 1975. Roly Weekes.

FIVE

The Bird class tankers, 1959–1962

BP Tankers had a history of naming classes of its tankers after specific themes, such as merchant naval or military ranks, trees etc (ie: *British Navigator, British Commander, British Beech*). Each ship within a certain class averaged a similar capacity tonnage, developing the fortunes of the parent company according to the vagrancies and whims of national and international oil markets. One such classification included the 13 tankers named, seemingly haphazardly, after popular British birds, with the (seemingly bizarre) addition of the New Zealand kiwi.

The class contained ships of general-purpose 'handy' sized capacity, capable of transporting multi-grade cargoes averaging 15/16,000 sdwt, and they were constructed in various British shipyards from 1959 to 1962. As the transportation of crude developed into the more financially viable larger tankers, these smaller-capacity ships were used increasingly for the vast range of products carried by the company. With an overall length averaging 525.5 feet, beam 69–70 feet and laden draught of around 30 feet, the ships were versatile and manoeuvrable, and could easily access the smaller refinery jetties so often situated in fairly shallow tidal waters. The first six tankers were each built to the order of the BTC and transferred to Clyde Charter Company upon completion, reverting to the parent company in 1972, whilst the remaining ships were built for and retained within the BTC fleet.

The first in the Bird class was *British Fulmar*. This tanker was designed to carry 15,983 sdwt on a mean summer draught of 29.4 feet at a speed of 14.5 knots. She was 524.8 feet overall, 495 feet bp, with a moulded breadth of 69 feet and moulded depth 37 feet. Her gross tonnage was 11,160. The cargo spaces were divided by two longitudinal and nine transversal bulkheads, giving 30 tanks. The four cargo pumps, operated from two pump rooms, each had a capacity around 480 tons per hour and, as the ship was equipped with heating coils, heavier grades of crude could be transported from some Nigerian (and other appropriate) oil ports. In keeping with many tankers of the time, she was also fitted with a stern discharge line. The class were fitted with the latest technological devices throughout on deck and below. Her latest deck machinery included steam-driven winches for mooring and handling the hose derricks, plus a capstan for handling both anchors.

The tanker class had accommodation for 61 European officers and crew, and an extra 14 when staffed by Indian ratings. The deck and engine room bhandaris had

The 15,983 sdwt tanker *British Fulmar* was launched in the Glasgow yards of A. Stephens Limited on 30 September 1958, and was completed in February 1959 for Clyde Charter Company. In keeping with other units of the BP Tanker fleet she reverted to the company in 1972, and the following year was transferred to Solamole Limited, where she continued trading under her own name. She was sold to a Panamanian owner in 1976 and renamed *Zhujiang*; resold two years later, and finally acquired by the Chinese People's Republic in 1979, to be renamed *Ta Ching 236*. Her chequered career continued, for in 1980 she was transferred internally within government departments and called *Da Qing 236*. It was under this name that she remained in service until, following a collision in October 1983, the ship finally sank in the China Seas. Fotoship.

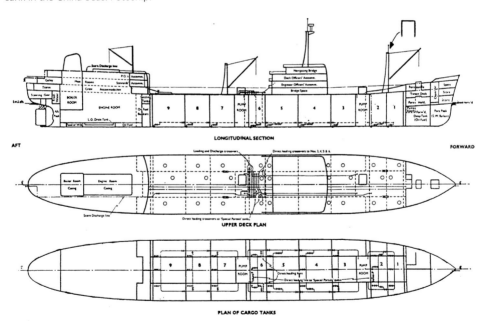

A GA plan of *British Fulmar* shows the configuration of cargo tanks and the disposition of the two pump rooms enabling a wide range of crude and refined oil parcels to be transported simultaneously. The main pump room was situated below the cargo pipe manifolds abaft the midships accommodation block. This controlled the direct cargo loading lines, whilst the forward room was restricted to controlling crossover lines handling cargoes in the special parcel tanks, 3, 4, 5 and 6. The 12-inch stern discharge line is taken up the poop front to the boat-house deck top above the PO's accommodation. The forward derrick was normally used for handling cargoes of drums containing a variety of lubricating oils, and to take heavy ship's gear, such as coils of mooring wires and ropes, into the bosun's stores.

their galleys aft, together with other crew amenities. Apart from the deck cadets, deck boys and catering boys, all personnel were berthed in single cabins planned with full consideration for comfort. Inevitably, the furniture and fittings reflected the general trend in these areas used ashore, with emphasis placed on providing that necessary spaciousness normally considered conducive to relaxation as antidotes to the demands of seafaring in quite demanding physical and climatic conditions. A swimming pool open to all hands was situated on the boat deckhouse aft, whilst the ships were fitted with a large recreation room aft for petty officers and ratings.

The engine room on these tankers was well designed. The ships were powered by 6- or 7-cylinder Stephen-Sulzer heavy oil engines of the type manufactured usually by the builders. The power output developed ranged between 7/800 bhp and gave a useful service speed of around 14–15.5 knots. Diesel oil was used only for close manoeuvring during stand-by and other situations requiring closer control of the ship's speed. On trials, the *British Fulmar* attained a speed of just over 16 knots with the engine developing 8,500 shp, although the fuel consumption at this normally 'emergency only' speed was considerably higher than that consumed during standard running.

In the following range of images taken on board *British Fulmar*, provided by courtesy of the major international shipping magazine *The Motor Ship*, an idea may be gained of the quality and modernity of accommodation and workplaces.

The officer's dining room on these tankers was fitted to the highest standards of comfort. Crisp linen tablecloths and napkins were the norm, with well-considered menus offered to crew, offering varied menus of dishes that were generally well prepared and cooked. A table was reserved for the senior officers' second sitting, whilst deck and engineering officers each had their own tables, as did cadets. The dining room and smoke room were situated aft on most tankers, invariably running down the port or starboard side of the accommodation block. These features were regarded by seafarers to serve as a form of compensation for the long periods of service on board tankers offering, as they did, limited (if any) shore leave owing to the unsocial, almost desolate, places where the refineries had to be located for safety reasons. An essential adornment in the dining rooms of all the company's ships were pictures of HM the Queen and the Duke of Edinburgh.

Although this view of the officers' smoke room in tankers of this class seems a little austere at first glance, the facilities offered proved remarkably conducive to relaxation. There was adequate room for popular games of cards and chess, but also for quiet reading and conversation. If deeper concentration was required then adjournment to a cabin was the better option. One positive aspect about serving in the Merchant Navy was the ability it forced on men to live with each other's foibles and idiosyncrasies! Invariably, a bar was provided, which was run on a casual basis with officers signing chits for their consumption. The 10 per cent discount for purchases through the officers' bond account, settled through salary arrangements made with the officers' bank account held in head office, made duty free spirits and cigarettes even cheaper; for example, 200 cigarettes cost 50p and a bottle of whisky about the same price – in the currency value of those days!

The crew mess room was invariably a friendly place, with separate tables provided for petty officers, leading hands and ratings. Invariably, a deck boy was told off to act as 'Peggy', serving the senior hands and keeping their single cabins clean. The same meals were cooked for officers and ratings, with the galley situated between the two messes. Separate tables were provided for senior petty officers and leading hands. Mealtimes were very much dependent on the arrivals and departures of any merchant ship respective to her loading and/or discharging ports, making it impossible to forecast when these could be served. The system nevertheless worked quite efficiently.

The bridge arrangement on the *British Fulmar* differed considerably, for this latter tanker retained the traditional separation between chart room and wheelhouse. This had both advantages and disadvantages. On the one hand, it was often easier to have the two separate, especially when concentrating on a difficult passage of navigation, but there was in contrast a bolted-on tendency to spend too much time away from the essential deck officer's task of maintaining at all times a proper lookout by visual and all available other means. The tables below the chart working space contained the folio of charts covering all waters in which the tanker might be called to operate.

The tail shaft arrangements of the *British Fulmar* powered by the 7-cylinder Sulzer oil engine. It has proved very difficult to find specific details of the engine arrangements and obtain archive shots of the engine-room area aboard this class of ships.

British Swift, the second in the class, was completed in October 1959 by Scott's Shipbuilding and Engineering Company at Greenock. In keeping with company policy, she was built for the BP Tanker Company and transferred immediately upon completion to Clyde Charter Company. In 1972 she reverted to BP Tanker Company, and the following year was transferred to Erynflex Limited, where she served under the same name until 1977, when she was sold to Noah Shipping Company of Honduras and renamed *Noah VI*. On 19 May 1982 after a collision with a larger tanker, *Cast Gull,* she proceeded to the port of Bahrain. Her subsequent history from this date remains uncertain, for she was eventually deleted from Lloyd's Register in 2000, classified as 'continued existence in doubt'. Roly Weekes.

This close-up shot of *British Gannet* shows the streamlining of the Bird class tankers given to the accommodation blocks and superstructure of the new breed of BP tankers. It offered not just a display of smartness and modernity, but hinted also at something of power. The straight 2-metre radar scanner above the wheelhouse midships block was a comparatively new indication of the modern range of radar sets available to merchant ships that replaced the cheese-shaped scanner popular for so many years. The goal-post masts forward offered some stronger support to the derricks but, more psychologically perhaps, again indicated a modern ship, which meant business. *British Gannet* was a typical 15,262 sdwt 'handy sized' ship completed in November 1959 and transferred to Clyde Charter Company; reverting to BP Tankers in 1972. She sailed with Crestaford from 1973 until 1976 when she was sold to United Freighters of Panama and renamed *Hanjiang*. In 1980, she was again sold to Panamanian interest and renamed *Newhaven*, and she continued in service until 1983, when she was run up on Gadani Beach and demolished. G. Brownell.

The 16,183 sdwt *British Kiwi* was fourth in the class. She was launched by Smith's Dock Company at Middlesbrough in July 1959 and was completed in January 1960. The vessel had an interesting history from that date for in 1976 she was converted to an offshore support vessel under the name *Forties Kiwi*, and was managed by BP Oil Development Company. In 1982 she was renamed *Coltair*. The ship was finally sold out of the BP fleet in 1986 when she went to Waterloo Shipping of Valetta, renamed *Kitty*. It was under this name that the vessel fell foul of an international overflux of tankers and was, like the numerous other merchant ships in various rivers and creeks around the UK coast, laid up. Under her present name she was moored in the River Blackwater, Essex, until 1989, when her career was finally terminated by her being scrapped in India. Roly Weekes.

British Robin at 15,450 sdwt came from Lithgow's yards in Port Glasgow, where she was launched in November 1959. In 1977 the ship was sold to a French owner, with whom she remained under the name *Lot* until 1983, when she was sold to Fal Bunkering Company in Dubai, who changed her name to *Fal XI*. Whilst awaiting demolition she was driven aground in heavy weather off the Pakistani coast, and eventually scrapped there in 1986. Roly Weekes.

The 15,939 sdwt *British Gull* was laid down at Harland and Wolff's Glasgow yards as *British Seagull*, but was launched in December under her new name. Completed in June 1960, the tanker served BP Tanker Company until 1976, when she was converted into a depot ship serving a number of laid-up BP tankers at Brunei Bay, being finally demolished at Kaohsiung in 1982. C.L. Reynolds.

Launched by Harland and Wolff's Belfast yards on 3 November 1959, the 15,866 sdwt *British Mallard* was completed in June 1960 and transferred to Clyde Charter Company. Reverting to BP Tanker fleet in 1972, she was sold to a French oil company who renamed her *Penhors*. Like *Robin*, she was resold in 1984 to the Fal Bunkering Company, whereupon she was renamed *Fal XII* and stationed at Dubai. Eventually, Fal sold her for demolition to Pakistani shipbreakers who ran her onto the beach at Gadani, to be scrapped in September 1987. World Ship Society.

British Curlew had a very chequered history. She was launched in January 1960 by Stephen and Sons of Glasgow and completed for BP Tanker Company in June, when she was transferred to Clyde Charter Company. The ship was 15,389 sdwt and powered by a 7-cylinder Sulzer oil engine manufactured by the builders which developed 7,500 bhp. In 1972 she was transferred back to BP Tanker Company, and remained there for four years until sold to Hemisphere Shipping Company (with Ocean Tramping Company as manager) of Hong Kong, who renamed her *Wenjiang*. In December 1980 the tanker was involved in the Gulf hostilities and from the outbreak was detained at Basra. She was damaged by shellfire in the steering flat, sustaining a 3-foot hole, and was later anchored in the Shatt al Arab waterway. Her subsequent movements and owners are uncertain, for she was deleted from Lloyd's Register in January 1992. C. L. Reynolds.

Harland and Wolff's Belfast yards saw the launching for BP Tanker Company of *British Cormorant* in January 1961, with completion on 6 July. She was 16,039 sdwt, and served the fleet until 1977 when she was sold to Trans-Ocean Maritime Shipping of Liberia and renamed *Oriental Endeavour*, but before she commenced trading she was renamed *Oriental Banker*. (This practice of rapidly renaming tankers was not such an uncommon procedure as might appear. In the days of easier access to Lloyd's Shipping Index – a bible much loved by ship professionals and enthusiasts alike – some ships were renamed as often as four times in a single day. The reasons for this procedure seem to have revolved around a constant reselling of vessels on the rapidly moving charter and ownership markets.) On 15 September 1983 the ship arrived under tow from Singapore to Thailand, where she was scrapped. C.L. Reynolds.

The 16,055 sdwt *British Osprey*, the tenth in the class, was completed by Harland and Wolff's Glasgow yards in January 1962 for BP Tanker Company. She had an overall length of 525.9 feet with a beam of 69.5 feet and was powered by 6-cylinder Burmeister and Wain oil engine developing 8,600 bhp. In 1977 she was sold to Pacific Tanker Transport Corporation registered in Liberia and renamed *Oriental Peace*. In 1982 she was laid up at Singapore for a period and renamed the following year *Allocean II*, and later that year was demolished at Kaohsiung. M. Lennon.

British Kestrel was eleventh in the class. She was launched by Hamilton's of Glasgow in October 1961 and completed in March 1962 for BP Tanker Company. The ship was 15,922 sdwt with an overall length of 535.3 feet and beam 69.4 feet. Her 6-cylinder oil engine was manufactured by Kincaid Company of Greenock and developed 8,600 bhp giving the tanker a speed of 15. 5 knots. In 1976 she was sold to the Peninsular Shipping Company of Hong Kong who renamed her *Sunjiang*; she remained in service with Peninsular until May 1983, when she was scrapped at Shanghai. World Ship Society.

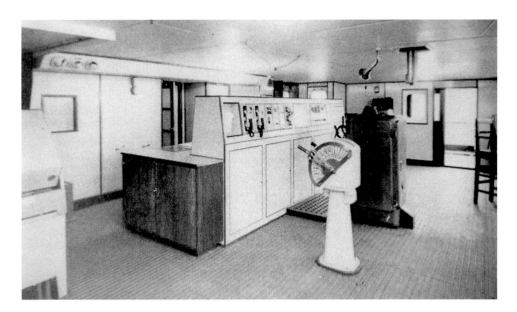

The modern light and airy combined wheelhouse and chartroom on the 1962 *British Kestrel* was similar to that on all the Bird class ships. It makes an interesting contrast with those situated aboard much earlier tankers. (See 3:5 *British Marquis* and 4.19 *British Destiny*.) The lighting in the chartroom aboard ships of all classes could be dimmed, helping the officer of the watch retain night vision, but still enabling essential chartwork to be carried out. One of the telephones on the bank aft of the telegraph was a direct emergency link to the engine room whilst the other was connected to the ship's automatic telephone exchange, which provided links to all important areas of the ship and individual officers' cabins. Two radars would have been installed in this area. One would offer a traditional relative motion display, and the other giving the newly provided true motion view, invariably fitted with some form of the automatic collision-avoidance plotting device being introduced into general service from the early 1960s. *The Motor Ship*.

The 16,116 sdwt *British Merlin* was completed at the Glasgow yards of Harland and Wolff for BP Tanker Company, and was immediately renamed *BP Enterprise*. In 1968 the vessel reverted to the name of *British Merlin* and remained with the company fleet until 1977 when under the name of *LSCO Basilan* she traded under the ownership of Luzon Stevedore Corporation in the Philippines. Working within the group of islands she was sold three years later to PNOC Shipping and Trading Company, who called her *PNOC Basilan*. Whilst on a local passage in November 1983, the ship experienced an onboard explosion that developed into a fire and she eventually sank off the west coast of Luzon. World Ship Society.)

British Cygnet was the last in the series of Bird class tankers. This 15,441 sdwt tanker was launched on 9 January 1962 by Harland and Wolff's Belfast yard and was completed on 7 June of that year for BP Tanker Company. In 1964 she was renamed *BP Endeavour* and three years later called *BP Explorer*. In 1969 she reverted to the name under which she had been completed. During the whole of this time she remained with BP Tanker Company. The ship was sold to Atlantic Tanker Transport of Liberia in 1977 and renamed *Oriental Unity*. In September 1982 she was demolished at Jakarta. A. Duncan.

SIX

A roller-coaster period: the 1960s

On the opening of the 1960s a significant factor directly affecting the tanker trade was the amendments introduced by Lloyd's Register of Shipping to the Rules for Oil Tanker Construction. These came into force on 7 July, and superseded the revisions made in 1930 and 1949 which had taken into consideration changes affecting the increasing size of tankers.

The new amendments arose almost as a side-effect of the Suez crisis, which had, along with economic factors, worked to accelerate the increased capacity of tankers. In the previous decade alone, for example, the deadweight tonnage of tankers had doubled, so whilst the new 1960 Rules applied to all tankers regardless of length, already an ever-growing number of vessels internationally exceeded 900 feet in length. This lay beyond parameters of the bending moments along the hull laid down in the 1949 Rules, when ships of up to 620 feet were adequate for general transportation.

In 1959, Daniel Ludwig had broken all records when he launched his 107,000 sdwt monster *Universe Apollo* with an overall length of 950 feet and laden draught of 48 feet. The revised 1960 rules dealt with the framing and internal structure along the hull by taking into consideration design features and hull stresses that permitted longer cargo capacity tanks to be built, with a corresponding reduction in their number. Fewer transversal bulkheads meant less constructional weight as well as simplified pumping arrangements, facilitating new advances using computerised cargo-handling technology. The effects meant that extra cargo could be carried. Combined with an increase in oil engine efficiency, the way was opened for modern computerised techniques which soon extended across an additional range of other shipboard facilities. Inevitably, a reduction in crew numbers followed, with corresponding less monies paid in crew wages, whilst fuel consumption – easily the biggest operating cost of most merchant vessels – was cut considerably.

It was probably no accident that in 1961 the main channel of the Suez Canal was dredged to a depth of 37 feet allowing laden tankers of up to 70,000 sdwt capacity to use the waterway. It remained at this depth until 1980, when dredging to 53 feet enabled access for large unladen tankers below 125,000 sdwt. The depth was again increased in 2001, this time to 62 feet, enabling unladen tankers of the V/ULCC class to make transit.

November 1962 saw completion of *British Cavalier* from the yards of J.L. Thompson of Sunderland. The vessel was ordered by, and entered into, the fleet of BP Tanker Company and at 54,577 sdwt, 32,417 grt, 760 feet overall was, for a brief moment, its largest ship. She was powered by two steam turbines manufactured by Parsons of Wallsend which developed 16,000 shp, giving a speed of 15.5 knots on a laden draught of 41 feet.

British Diplomat had the distinction of being the last tanker owned by the BP company to be built as a three-islander. She was launched in March 1963 by Ateliers et Chantiers de Dunkerque et Bordeaux at its Dunkirk yards for BP Tanker Company. She was 49,320 sdwt, 31,259 grt with an overall length of 747.9 feet and 99.33 feet beam. Her two steam turbines, geared to a single propeller shaft, were built by Ateliers et Chantiers de Bretagne, Nantes, and developed 17,800 shp, giving a service speed of 16.5 knots on a summer laden draught of 39.33 feet.

The first of the new-style construction tankers with the navigating bridge and all accommodation aft was the 54,788 sdwt *British Grenadier* launched in August 1962 by Vickers Armstrong yards at Barrow-in-Furness and completed in January 1963 for BP Tanker Company. The new arrangement of all accommodation aft proved a great relief to tanker deck officers, for being boarded above the cargo tanks had long proved a bone of contention, with numerous accidents occurring, often leading to severe loss of life when midships tanks had exploded. Certainly, fears expressed by some navigators and pilots that moving the bridge so far aft would have detrimental effects on navigational and ship-handling efficiency were soon proved groundless. Accompanying the new style of construction was the first fitting of a newly designed 360° slewing crane serving the manifolds amidships. This replaced the twin derricks, but still performed the same function of keeping the weight of pipe connections between ship and shore off the railings.

British Cavalier was launched in June 1962 by Thompson's shipyard of Sunderland, and completed the following November. At 54,577 sdwt she was the largest capacity ship in the BP Tanker Company fleet. Her overall length was 760 feet with a beam of 97.3 feet and laden draught of 41 feet. She served the company until December 1975, when she arrived at Kaohsiung, to be demolished the following month. World Ship Society.

British Diplomat was launched from the Dunkirk yards of Atelier et Chantiers de Dunkerque et Bordeaux on 12 March 1963 and completed for the BP Tanker Company in June 1963. She was 747.9 feet length overall with a 99.33 feet beam. She was the last three-island vessel owned by the company, and she served until November 1975 when she arrived at the Sing Chen Yung Iron and Steel Corporation yards in Kaohsiung, where work began on her demolition the following month. A Duncan.

The *British Venture* was another tanker from Hawthorn's yards, where she was completed in April 1963 as the second all-aft vessel. She was 35,700 sdwt, 678 feet overall length and 86.25 feet beam. Her claim to fame, however, was holding the record as the first large British tanker to be powered by diesel engines. She had originally been intended as a (by now conventional) steam turbine ship, but company policy in 1960 investigating comparisons between various methods of propulsion planned for this 'handy' class ship to be refitted prior to launching. Her engine was also a first, for it would be the first modern large-bore 8-cylinder diesel engine built in the UK. This was a Hawthorn-Sulzer 8 RD90 type, having a power rating of 14,200 bhp giving a service speed around 15.5 knots. This also featured a uniquely BP-designed highly advanced (for the time) system of optimum performance exhaust gas heat recovery. This resulted in the saving and re-use of 35 per cent heat that would otherwise be discharged into the atmosphere.

Undoubtedly the star of the capacity show in 1963 was *British Mariner*. She continued the trend of increasing the tonnage capacity in line with the policy of potentially routeing tankers around the Cape in the event of further problems closing the Suez Canal. This ship was built by John Brown's Clydebank yards and was 74,635 sdwt, 43,605 grt, with an overall length of 815 feet, making her (for an all too brief while) the largest tanker constructed in the UK. Inevitably, the ship contained many of the latest techniques, particularly regarding her engine room. The distance from bridge to bow was 650 feet, slightly below the 665 overall length of the 1957 *British Glory*.

British Mariner was the first BP ship to be powered by a set of the two newly designed Pametrada steam turbine double-reduction engines geared to a single shaft developing 20,000 shp, giving a laden service speed of around 15.5 knots on a laden summer draught

The 54,788 sdwt *British Grenadier* was the first BP company tanker to be constructed with all accommodation aft. She was launched on 16 August 1962 at the Barrow-in-Furness yards of Vickers Armstrong, and completed the following January. The tanker was 760 feet in overall length with a moulded beam of 97.5 feet, and was powered by two steam turbines constructed by the builders, developing 16,000 shp giving a service speed of 15.5 knots on a laden summer draught of 42 feet. Following a short period when she was laid up in Singapore the vessel was subsequently sold, and eventually scrapped at Kaohsiung, in April 1976. Roly Weekes.

British Venture was the second all-accommodation-aft tanker in the fleet. She was completed for the BTC in April 1963 at 38,112 sdwt with an overall length of 678 feet (640 feet bp), beam 86.3 feet and depth 50 feet, and a summer draught of 37.5 feet. Her cargo configuration consisted of three sets of ten tanks with port and starboard 4 and 5 wings arranged for clean seawater ballast only. This had its own separate pumping system, although main centre tanks 1,3 and 5 plus 2, 3, 6 and 8 wing tanks were assigned for extra ballast water in the event of severe weather and sea conditions. Most well-found and well-handled ships could readily face storm force winds in excess of 12 on the Beaufort scale during any sea passage, but flooding some cargo tanks helped maintain hull stability and enhanced steering. This tanker had three 1,000 tons/hr cargo pumps, with one 200 tons/hour stripping pump, and one 750 tons/hr ballast pump. A further interesting feature was her fitting with automated ullage gauges in all cargo tanks. She served the company until she was demolished at Kaohsiung in May 1978. A. Duncan.

BP Tanker Company's *British Mariner* was completed by John Brown's Clydeside shipyards on 9 October 1963 following her launching the previous April. At 74,636 sdwt capacity with an overall length of 815 feet and moulded beam 113 feet, she was the largest tanker built in the UK. She was also the first to be fitted with two sets of Pametrada steam turbine engines geared to a single shaft which developed 20,000 shp giving the vessel a service speed of 15.5 knots on a summer draught of 43.5 feet. She was the first company tanker to be fitted with an inert gas system, and separate air-conditioned self-contained engine room from which could be operated all relevant machinery essential to powering the vessel, and operating cargo and ballast pumps. *British Mariner* served the fleet until November 1975, when she was broken up in Kaohsiung. Roly Weekes.

of 43.5 feet. A further unique development of this ship was the air-conditioned, sound-proofed and self-contained engine control system enabling normal watch-keeping to be maintained without the necessity of entering the engine room. This was part of company policy that would be designed eventually to facilitate fully automated tankers, with bridge control of the engines. The tanker was also the first BP vessel to be fitted with an inert gas system (IGS) undoubtedly (and few would argue) the greatest tanker safety device of the 20th century. The Sun Oil Company in the USA had developed this system and used it since 1932, but without firing the immediate imaginations of a wider international shipping industry at that time – due, apparently, to fears over its improper use.

British Mariner followed the traditional tank configuration of Isherwood's 2 longitudinal bulkheads with 12 transversals creating 39 tanks. Three port and three starboard wing tanks at Numbers 4, 5 and 6 were designated for clean water ballast only, with a separate pump that worked at 1,500 tons/hour. Cargo was handled by three centrifugal pumps, each with a capacity of 2,600 tons/hour, and a stripping pump operating at 250 tons/hour. It was by the time this ship was in service that BP were regularly using Götaverken's electronic analogue computers which were tailor-made for each tanker and assisted in calculating hull stresses whilst loading, unloading and transferring cargoes.

A significant tanker built for BP Tanker Company in 1964 was the 75,578 sdwt *British Ensign*. She was launched at Cammell Laird's Birkenhead shipyards on 4 October 1963 and completed in April 1964. She was the first company ship to take maximum advantage of Lloyd's Register's 1960 Revised Rules for Oil Tanker Construction, introduced shortly

British Mariner on the slipway prior to launching. The tracing chains along the tanker's side helped control the momentum once she was released on the slipway, before the tugs could take greater control over her movements. BP Plc.

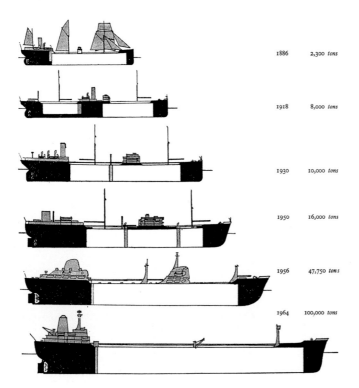

1886	2,300 *tons*
1918	8,000 *tons*
1930	10,000 *tons*
1950	16,000 *tons*
1956	47,750 *tons*
1964	100,000 *tons*

This virtually self-explanatory diagram shows the enormous increase in overall length and capacity of tankers in a period of less than 80 years. The development of streamlining in hull contours can be plainly seen, along with that of the funnel, and the gradual movement aft of the navigating bridge and all accommodation. These designs have subsequently been dwarfed by the advent of the VLCC and ULCC.

Two views of *British Ensign*, built in 1964. This 75,578 sdwt, 43,335 grt tanker entered BP Tanker Company fleet in April 1964. The ship was launched by Cammell Laird's Birkenhead yards and was 815.17 feet in length overall, with a beam of 113 feet. She was the first BP vessel to take advantage of Lloyd's Register 1960 Revised Rules for Oil Tanker Construction, being constructed with a lesser number but longer cargo tanks. (She was the second BP ship to carry this name. Her predecessor, with a capacity of 10,860 sdwt, had been built in 1917 by Armstrong, Whitworth and Company of Newcastle, and served the company until 1937, when she was scrapped.) This *British Ensign* served in the fleet until January 1976, when she was demolished at Kaohsiung. Both photos G. Brownell.

beforehand, which permitted her to have longer oil tanks. Like *British Mariner*, which had entered into service the previous year, she was fitted with Pametrada steam turbine engines, developing the same power of 20,000 shp and offering a similar service speed, of around 15.5 knots on a summer draught of 44.1 feet.

~~~~~~

Seeing the two ships together enables a number of obvious historical comparisons to be made. The 351.5-foot, 6,089-ton *British Trader* was completed in November 1921 in the Glasgow yards of William Beardmore and served in the BTC, then BP Tanker, fleets as late as 1953, when she was sold to the London-Greek firm of Cheam Shipping Limited,

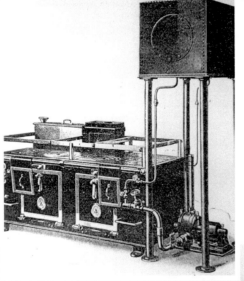

The complexity of the 1965-style galley fitted on board *British Willow* makes an interesting contrast with the extreme simplicity of that fitted in 1921 to *British Trader*. Yet within their parameters, both were very much functional norms of their times. The *Tanker and Bulk Carrier*, and *Fairplay Shipping* magazines.

British Willow was a 20,750 sdwt, 561 feet overall vessel launched by James Laing and Sons' Newcastle shipyards in October 1964 for the BP Tanker Company. She was completed in May 1965 and, a few days later, transferred to BP Thames Tanker Company Limited with whom she served until 1983. The ship was then sold to Castle Shipping Company who renamed her *Newcastle* and transferred her to Dilmun Marine Services of Gibraltar for management. Five years later she was sold to a Maltese company, Flamingo Shipping, who called her *Flamingo I* and arranged for her to be managed by a local firm. The ship was reported as demolished in 1994. J. Prentice.

who renamed her *Flisvos*. It in turn sold her two years later to a Peruvian company who renamed her *Manco Capac*. The history of the ship has become lost from that point, for she was subsequently deleted by Lloyd's Register in 1961, some 40 years following her launch. Roly Weekes.

~~~~~

1965 saw a further milestone in the history of the BTC fleet, with the launch of *British Admiral*. At 111,274 sdwt she was the first company tanker to exceed the 100,000 sdwt mark and at the time was the largest ship constructed in Europe. The launch on 17 March 1965 at Vickers Limited yards, Barrow-in-Furness, celebrated in style the 50th anniversary of the founding of the transport arm of Anglo-Persian Oil Company, with HM Queen Elizabeth II performing the ceremony. The ship was completed the following August, and within a few days embarked on her maiden voyage. Although built to the order of BP Tanker Company the ship was transferred just prior to her sailing to BP Tyne Tanker Company.

This impressive tanker, at 917.5 feet length overall, had a beam of 128.41 feet and moulded depth of 51.9 feet. She traded largely from eastern Mediterranean oil pipelines to Milford Haven in south Wales, or Finnart in Scotland, and during her first year of service transported over one million tons of crude. The company had again benefited from the revised Rules for Oil Tanker Construction by reducing the number of tanks to seven sets of three. Of the twenty-one tanks, four were designed for water ballast with their separate pumping and line system with the by now conventional number of centre tanks set aside for sea ballast in conditions of extremely rough weather. Her single pump room contained four cargo pumps each with a capacity of 1,860 tons/hour and two ballast pumps, each with a capacity of 1,500 tons/hour. The fully automated Japanese-designed engine room was the first of its kind in the world, and marked the start of what would prove to be rapid expansion in computerisation. All valves were push-button operated and worked by a card system inserted by the chief officer, based on calculations derived from the ship's Sperry/Sintef cargo loading/discharging computer. The valves closed automatically once cargo had reached the predetermined level. This important consideration helped prevent the possibility of all too human error under extreme pressure, which had on some occasions caused an overspill. A free-flow discharge system was another innovative and unique feature of the cargo-handling system, in which hydraulically operated pipe lines and bulkhead valves allowed cargo to flow into the aftermost tank, from where it could be pumped ashore. The light displacement of the ship was 23,000 tons.

Her engines attracted the attention of the world's maritime press especially as this department of the tanker was fitted with highly automated complex control systems. Vickers also built her 25,000 shp double-reduction steam turbines which, geared to a single shaft, gave the vessel a service speed of 15.5 knots on a summer draught of 49 feet.

BP's flagship, *British Admiral*, under way on her maiden voyage. This 111,274 sdwt, 61,768 grt tanker had an overall length of 917.5 feet, a beam of 128.41 feet, and a depth of 51.9 feet. She was completed at Vickers' Barrow-in-Furness yards in Cumbria during August 1965 and was the largest ship built in Europe. The ship's two steam turbines were linked to a single shaft and together developed 25,000 shp, giving a service speed of 15.5 knots on a draught of 49 feet. She served the fleet until July 1976, when she was demolished at Kaohsiung, BP Plc.

The launching of *British Admiral* occurred on 17 March 1965 and was performed by HM Queen Elizabeth II, attended by senior company officials and local dignitaries. Tugs have already brought the ship up, controlling her momentum and preventing any hindering of the main shipping channels. BP Plc.

The magazine *Tanker Times* commented on this ship:

This is undoubtedly the most advanced vessel in the BP fleet, the complexity of her control system being reflected in the composition of the 43-man crew, nearly 50% of whom are officers … the BP fleet now consists of 100 ships aggregating 2,700,000 tons dwt.

It was also in 1 that the company took delivery of a further eight tankers: seven 13,500 sdwt Tree class, and the first of four 64,000 sdwt tankers, the *British Commerce*.

British Argosy, a near-sister ship of *British Admiral,* was completed by Swan Hunter's Newcastle yards on 2 July 1966. The tanker was 112,786 sdwt, 62,427 grt, with an overall length of 920.75 feet and a 128.5-foot moulded beam. The moulded depth was 66 feet. Her two steam turbines, manufactured by Wallsend Slipway Company, developed 25,000 shp giving a speed of 15.5 knots on a summer draught of 51.8 feet.

The navigational facilities aboard *British Admiral* were (not unexpectedly) state of the art for the time. The layout in the wheelhouse would set the pattern for all later very large tankers in the company fleet, but at the time was revolutionary. She was fitted with two Kelvin-Hughes radar sets, and a Sperry gyroscope compass. The ship could be controlled in an emergency from the Decca Arkas steering console whose inner wheel could override any predetermined course that had been set, and the vessel was fitted with an off-course alarm, generally set to operate at 10° port or starboard, and a course recorder. The main true motion radar set was fitted with an automatic anti-collision plotting device. *Tanker and Bulk Carrier* magazine

The fo'c'sle head of *British Admiral* shows the modern 100-ton steam anchor windlass that stood over 9 feet in height and 40 feet over the warp ends. It was capable of an anchor breakout pull of 110 tons when both steam engines worked at 100 tons/square inch; these were situated below the fo'c'sle head. Also visible are two of the ship's eight steam mooring winches with their drums, each capable of pulling 19 tons at the slow speed of 120 feet/minute, essential for safety during berthing operations. The 'dollies' adjacent to the windlasses are designed to assist the mooring wires and ropes to be led from the winches over the ship's side, via the bollards. These and all deck machinery were provided by tanker experts Clarke Chapman and Company. *The Motor Ship*.

May 1967 saw fulfilment of BP management's fears when Egypt entered into another dispute with Israel, encouraging Colonel Nasser to order closure of the Suez Canal. Supported by other Arab nations, including Libya and Algeria, an oil embargo was imposed upon all countries trading with Israel. This included Britain and America, and led yet again to the re-routeing of tankers around the Cape. The move was cemented in June by the complete closure of the canal by a series of blockships, following the Six Day war between Egypt and Israel.

On this occasion, the canal remained closed until September 1967, leading all nations relying on Arabian oil to seek for alternative sources of supply, invariably from Indonesia and Venezuela. Nigerian oilfields remained out of commission due to an internal conflict and civil unrest.

A rare shot of one of *British Admiral's* wing cargo swash tanks. The photograph indicates the strength built into these structures. The bottom girders and frames can be seen clearly, along with horizontal stiffeners and webs supporting the longitudinal bulkheads, side shell vertical transversals, horizontal brackets fixed at the top and bottom. BP Plc.

British Commerce was the first of four 69,000 sdwt tankers launched in July 1964 for the BP Tanker Company from the slipways of J.L. Thompson and Sons in Sunderland. She was completed in May 1965, and in September of that year was transferred to the Tyne Tanker Company. The vessel was 815.9 feet in length overall with a moulded beam of 43.3 feet, and her 9-cylinder Sulzer-type oil engine was manufactured by G. Clarke and North-Eastern Marine Limited, Sunderland. This developed 207,000 shp giving a service speed of 15 knots on a draught of 40.7 feet. In January 1983 she was scrapped at Kaohsiung. J. Brownell.

The same year saw five tankers entering company service with the launching of three 68,000 sdwt tankers, *British Captain*, *British Centaur* and *British Commodore*. They were each around 817 feet in length overall and 108 feet moulded beam. Apart from *British Captain*, which was powered by two steam turbines developing 20,000 shp, the other two were fitted with 9-cylinder Burmeister and Wain oil engines developing 18,000 shp. All three vessels had a laden service speed around 15–15.5 knots.

The year 1966 marked a major change in direction concerning the fortunes of BP Corporation affecting its transport arm, BP Shipping. The directors exercised much of the business foresight and acumen, a hallmark of the company's history, through which they had assessed major reviews of world events. All areas were included, with specific emphasis on the current and possible future world demands for crude and refined oils. This involved international production and shipping capacity, and against their findings assessment was made of how best the company's fleet of tankers might be involved.

The benefits arising from trading two tankers in excess of 100,000 sdwt, *British Admiral* and *British Argosy*, were already paying dividends. This included not only transporting greater cargo capacity per vessel but also benefits derived from reductions in operating costs, especially as fuel and diesel consumption remained the greatest single factor affecting

Left and above – The two initial shots demonstrate methods of shipbuilding prevalent in the United Kingdom at the time of the completion of the *British Argosy*, in July 1966, from Swan Hunter's Tyneside yards. With the vessel nearing completion, the mass of material cluttering the main deck fore and aft shows this impressive structure taking its final shape. Undoubtedly, she was a fine ship with streamlined lines, and lamp-posts unique to tankers of this size ...

   ... The tanker was 112,786 sdwt with an overall length of 920.75 feet. She was built for BP Tanker Company with whom she served until 1976 when, just ten years after her maiden voyage, demolition commenced at the Nan Feng Steel Enterprise Company in Kaohsiung in September. All photographs Roly Weekes.

April 1965 saw the launch of the 67,994 sdwt *British Captain* by the Cammell Laird yards at Birkenhead for BP Tanker Company, with completion the following January. This impressive tanker was handed over to Tanker Charter Company shortly before embarking on her maiden voyage, and in 1967 reverted to BP Tanker Company. In 1972 she was again transferred back to Tanker Charter, with whom she remained until sold in 1976 to United Maritime Enterprises of Greece and renamed *Halcyon Med*. Within three years the vessel was sold to the Greek North Star Shipping Company and in 1982 was laid up at Aliveri, Euboea Island, Greece. In February 1985 she was demolished at Kaohsiung. Roly Weekes.

running such large tankers. Fewer crew provided additional advantages, probably because it was the second-greatest cost. This occurred not only in wages but also catering and the expenses involved in flying crew exchanges across the globe. In addition, this was a period of shortages in competent officers and ratings which had led to increasing demands across all shipping companies for qualified men and women. It resulted in the introduction of six-monthly contracts for company officers and petty officers, together with an offer of berths to officers' wives (back then, the officers were still all male).

Inevitably these factors encouraged company minds to think along lines of ships having even greater capacity and in 1967 BP Tanker Company made the first in a number of significant moves. It registered a new company, BP Medway Tanker Company Limited, that was to play a major part in the fleet's history, and orders were placed for a series of 15 Very Large Crude Carriers, (VLCCs, or 'true' supertankers), each exceeding 200,000 sdwt capacity. British yards were invited to submit contracts but – for the first time in company history, because the yards had failed to cope with new ship construction technology and were beset by union difficulties – these were unable to compete with the cost and delivery times offered by Japanese and other European yards.

The idea at the time was that such large vessels should sail to Middle Eastern oilfields through the Suez Canal, and return fully laden, on a forecast draught of around 80+ feet, by rounding Cape Agulhas. They would take stores as necessary from a launch whilst passing Cape Town. In this way fuel consumption would be minimised over the 22,000-mile return trip, which could help considerably in keeping VLCCs economically viable.

There were already precedents upon which the directors could base their forecasts, for the same year, 1968, had seen Daniel Ludwig taking delivery of the world's first Ultra Large Crude Carrier, ULCC *Universe Ireland*, at a staggering 326,585 sdwt. This giant was the first of six ships exceeding 300,000 sdwt ordered from two Japanese yards. Already, even after such a brief interval, reports of large profits being accrued by successful owning and managing mammoth tankers were seeping into boardrooms across the world, creating the necessary momentum to a number of world ship owners, thus motivating a surge in orders for VLCCs.

Harland and Wolff's Belfast yard launched *British Centaur* on 15 June 1965 for the BP Tanker Company. Her completion was in the following January, for Tanker Charter Company. This 67,697 sdwt tanker was transferred back to BP Tanker Company in 1967 and in 1972 reverted to Tanker Charter Company; it is rare for those outside the boardroom to understand the machinations underpinning the reasons affecting the decisions concerning inter-transference of any ships, let alone the vagrancies occurring in the tanker markets. She was sold to Harrisons (Clyde) of Glasgow in 1983 and renamed *Earl of Skye*, and in June 1984 she arrived at Ulsan, South Korea, for demolition. Both photos BP Plc.

Daniel Ludwig's ULCC *Universe Ireland*. Clearly not a BP Tanker, but included here as she represented at the time a vessel of seemingly outlandish dimensions. The ship was 327,000 sdwt with an overall length of 1,133 feet, 1,089 feet bp, 176 feet beam and moulded depth 105 feet, and she was delivered from the Japanese yards of Ishikawajima-Harima Heavy Industries in 1968. She was powered by two double-reduction steam turbine engines that each generated 187,000 bhp serving two propellers. This gave the tanker a service speed of 15 knots on a summer draught of 81 feet and offered greater manoeuvrability, except perhaps in the views of some pilots and masters, at lower running speeds. Her size restricted her to the newly built terminals at Okinawa, Bantry Bay in Ireland, and Port Hawkesbury in Canada, until the Louisiana Offshore Oil Port had completed construction and was available for regular service. *Universe Ireland* was sold to Greek owner Avin Oil Episkopi in 1980; resold the following year to Hagi Episkopi, also Greek, and then in 1984, following her transfer to Episkopi, she was demolished in Kaohsiung. A. Duncan.

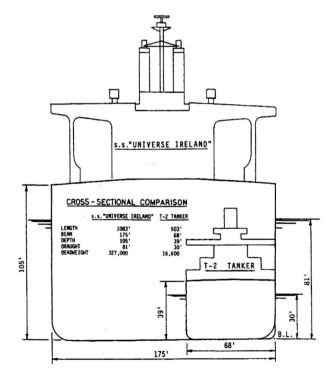

A self-explanatory comparative cross-sectional diagram between *Universe Ireland* and a standard 16,000 sdwt T2 tanker, of which BP chartered a considerable number.

Continuing 1966 boardroom decisions regarding the fleet of product carriers saw BP Tanker Company casting its building nets more widely worldwide, by taking delivery from Australian yards of the 19,500 sdwt *BP Endeavour* upon her completion in September 1967. The following year, from the Swedish yards of Eriksberg MV Ab yards at Gothenburg, three tankers were accepted, near-sister ships to the 20,000 sdwt *British Liberty, British Loyalty* and *British Security*. The Swedish vessels were each around 550 feet overall length with a beam of 73–80 feet. Each was powered by a 6-cylinder B&W oil engine developing 7,500 bhp giving a service speed around 16 knots on a summer laden draught of 32 feet.

BP by this time owned 132 tankers totalling over 4 million tons deadweight capacity, were long-term chartering over 5 million tons, and had placed orders for numerous new buildings that were in various stages of construction and completion. Things were looking favourable in other areas with the discovery of oil by BP's Exploration Arm at Prudhoe Bay in Alaska, and steps methodically taken to exploit this to full capacity. A chain of 9,700 retail garage outlets and two oil refineries had been acquired throughout the USA from Sinclair Oil and Atlantic Richfield, thus contributing to greater diversity.

The fleet meanwhile continued to grow, meeting the world's increasing demands for oil. In 1968, three tankers between 19,000 and 23,000 sdwt were delivered. Two came from Swedish yards and the other, a sister ship to the *BP Endeavour*, which also came from Australian ship builders. These were followed in 1969 with a further two of similar tonnage from Sweden, and two of around 24,400 sdwt from Split in Yugoslavia.

British Liberty was launched on 15 February 1968 by Eriksberg MV Ab yards in Gothenburg, and completed the following May. She was 24,000 sdwt with an overall length of 556.5 feet and beam of 81.5 feet. She was powered by 6-cylinder Burmeister and Wain oil engine developing 7,500 bhp, giving a service speed around 16 knots on a summer draught of 31.3 feet. In 1981 she was sold to French owner Société d'Armement et de Transport and Compagnie Marseillaise de Réparations, and renamed *Folgoet*. The tanker remained with that owner until 15 September 1992, when she had an extensive lay-up in Marseilles. After January 1996, she was transferred to the St Vincent and Grenadines registry, and in March the same year was beached at Alang, India, and demolished. M. Dippy.

18 December 1968 saw the first BP tanker ship ordered from Yugoslavian yards. This was the 24,386 sdwt *British Unity* and she was completed in July 1969 by the builders, Brodogradiliste | Tvornica Dizel Motora, at Split. She was followed six months later by a second vessel from the same yards, *British Unity*, 558 feet overall length with beam 81.5 feet, powered by a 6-cylinder B&W engine manufactured under licence by the builders. Her 7,500 bhp oil engine gave her a service speed around 16 knots on a summer draught of 31 feet. She served the fleet until 1981, when she was sold to a Panamanian owner and renamed *Sebastiana*. In 1985 she was resold to Goldfin Corporation in the Bahamas and renamed *Silver Cloud*. She remained with Goldfin until 1987, when she was resold to Rubiomar SA under Panamanian registration and renamed *Noel Bay*. The vessel remained there for two years and was then sold to a Maltese owner and renamed *Bayonne*. January 1994 saw her anchored off Alang and finally demolished on its beach. Roly Weekes.

SEVEN

Trading successes of the early 1970s

By 1969 the fortunes of the BP conglomerate company were at a high; the period was indeed its golden age. Eric Drake, the company chairman, was able to declare in a press release not only that the company fortunes for 1968 were 'very encouraging', but to build on this success, he hinted 'we may be on the threshold of new and exciting developments'. J.H. Bamberg (in his comprehensively researched company history, Vol. 2, p. 279) described BP as:

> the third largest oil marketer in Europe … selling gasoline to through more than 26,000 filling stations in Western Europe, from Scandinavia in the north to Greece and Turkey in the south.

British Dart was launched on 22 March 1972 from the yards of Eriksberg MV Ab. (Lindholmen Division) at Gothenburg for BP Tanker Company. She was completed six months later, and served the company until 1976 when the management was transferred to the Irano-British Ship Service Company Limited. The 25,245 sdwt tanker was 15,605 grt with a between-perpendiculars length of 562.5 feet and a beam of 82.2 feet. She was powered by a 6-cylinder oil engine manufactured by Uddevallavarvet AB in Uddevalla, Sweden. In 1986 the vessel was sold to National Iranian Tanker Company who renamed her *Minab III* and with whom she sailed until sold for demolition in March 2002. Her subsequent disposal is not recorded. In this shot the ship is showing the colours of NITC. Roly Weekes.

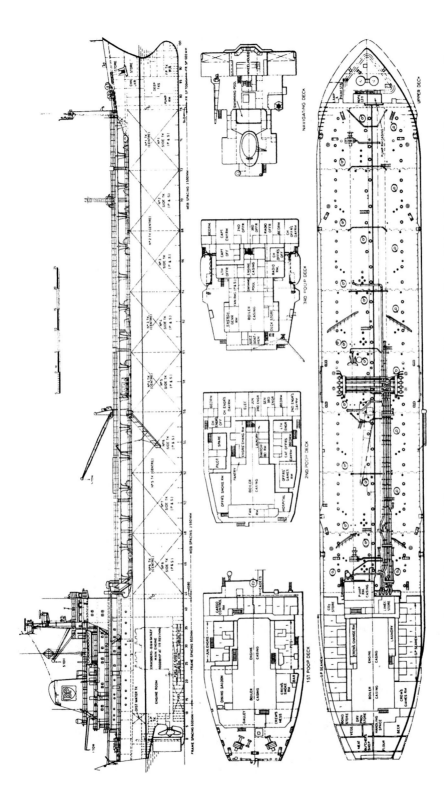

The GA plan of *British Dart* was reflected, with occasional differences, across the remainder of the series. Clearly visible is the forepeak ballast tank surmounting deep tanks for fuel oil; a forward pump room, and the traditional two longitudinal bulkheads giving eight cargo tanks subdivided into sets of centre and wings. Provision of the V or ram bulb to the stem, raked fo'c'sle and transom stern, with streamlined accommodation block and funnel contributed towards the appearance of a sleek, modern and fast vessel, enhanced by the introduction of a slightly projected conning section to the wheelhouse.

The hydraulic pipe handling crane, provided by a Dutch company, Schot, had a 5-ton swl, and was placed on the centre line amidships, adjacent to the cargo discharge manifolds. A second Schot 5-ton crane on the port side of the wheelhouse, abaft the mainmast, was used to handle engine room and deck equipment. Then a 1-ton Schot, situated on the starboard aft quarter of the boat deck was useful to bring the ship's stores on board. To assist cargo working at night, deck lighting was provided by the lamp-post above Number 2 tank, supplemented by powerful lamps fitted either side of the accommodation.

It was not only in the North Sea and across the Channel that the company flourished, for less than a year following its first production the BP Oilfield at Prudhoe Bay in Alaska was proving an unqualified success, along with BP's other interests globally. In 1970 at Forties the largest oilfield in the North Sea was discovered, although it would be a further five years before optimum production commenced. That year BP merged its American assets with the Standard Oil Company of Ohio, and in that same year the company owned 75 per cent of Nigeria's crude oil output. Libyan oil, meanwhile, discovered as long ago as 1957, remained productive.

The fact that demand for worldwide transport had increased accordingly was reflected equally in the growth of the BP tanker fleet. As seen in Chapter 6, while orders had been placed for a fleet of VLCCs, which were already being launched from Japanese shipyards, the company's fleet of product and smaller crude carriers continued unabated. Their routes remained worldwide with that familiar BP funnel prominent in every continent and on many major sea routes.

The compact raised fo'c'sle head of *British Dart*. Headlines leading moorings on the port side from both forward bollards can be seen. Both steam windlasses for the anchors, with independently operated drums for warps, were provided by Helsingborg's Varv Company. The carpenter, or a senior cadet, usually operated this gear during stand-by under the direction of the chief officer. *The Motor Ship*.

The modern wheelhouse of *British Dart* was combined with the chartroom. This was becoming an increasingly popular feature on modern tankers and obviated the necessity of leaving watch-keeping for longer periods by having to visit a separate chart area. The navigating equipment was laid out in an easy to use fashion. The centre of three consoles contained the popularly reliable Decca Autopilot 751 series, steering wheel and, on the starboard side, the Jungner main engine bridge control system, with a telegraph used when the engine room was staffed during stand-by operations. Push-button controls were incorporated, operating engine-room alarms, control change-over switches, appropriate gauges and an engineer call-out telephone. The port side console was separated by a Decca Relative Motion 425 radar set and was geared to hold a Rediphon vhf set, and Simrad depth indicator. The starboard console housed telephone systems to all important stations on the vessel including officers' cabins and the engine-room movement recorder. *The Motor Ship*.

The galley ranges and working areas on *British Dart* were clean and modern, incorporating an electric oven, chip fryer, dish washer, and meat-slicing machines. *The Motor Ship*.

British Test was in many respects a sister ship to *British Dart*. She came from the same Swedish yards and was constructed with similar dimensions and history. When sold to NITC, she was renamed *Minab IV*, but her fate is better documented than that of *Dart*, for she was beached at Alang on 16 April 2004 and subsequently demolished. M. Dippy.

The third in the River series of product tankers was *British Humber*. This tanker was launched by Brodogradiliste, Split, in (the then) Yugoslavia, indicating that the company was continuing to spread its orders across a number of European yards. Her dimensions were similar to others in the class and this vessel was completed in February 1973 for BP Tanker Company. In 1985 she was transferred to BP International and registered in the Bahamas, with BP Shipping Limited appointed manager, and was renamed *BP Humber*. In 1991 the tanker was sold to Roma Leasing, Italy, who renamed her *Akradina*; she stayed there for five years until resold to Navigazione Alta Italia of Naples, who appointed Beam Gestioni S.r.l. as manager. This company ran the vessel until 1998 when, retaining both her manager and her name, she was resold to Navigazione Montanari. The vessel was beached and demolished at Alang in May 2000. M. Dippy.

British Tay was launched on 23 January 1973 by Eriksberg of Gothenburg and completed the following June for BP Tanker Company. In 1992 she was sold to TCP Marine Shipping Company of Panama who renamed her *South Wind I*. Two years later, it sold her to another Panama company, International Oil Tanking, who appointed Eurasian Shipping and Management as manager. In July 1997, the tanker was reported anchored off Alang, awaiting demolition. Roly Weekes. .

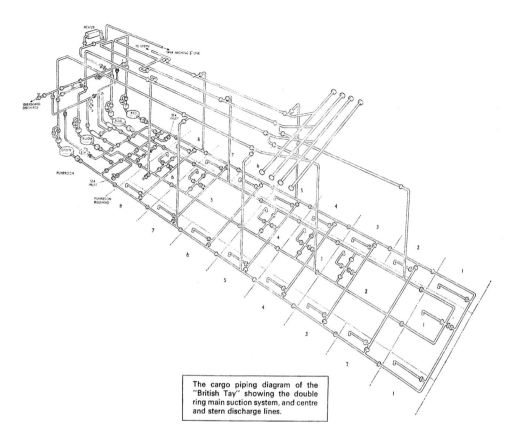

The cargo piping diagram of the "British Tay" showing the double ring main suction system, and centre and stern discharge lines.

The cargo piping diagram of *British Tay* showing main systems from the four steam turbine-driven Worthington-Simpson centrifugal cargo pipes, each with a capacity of 750 tonnes/hour. It was BP practice to afford a different colour system to each cargo pump and its associated suction and discharge lines. This meant all valves were clearly colour-coded at a glance by either red, blue, yellow or green, and led to either manifold or stern loading/discharge connections. Crossover lines assisted distribution of cargo during loading/discharge operations helping maintain stability of the ship. Tank distribution on this tanker varied slightly from the *British Dart* and others in that she had six centre tanks and sixteen wings. The centres comprised four long and two shorter cargo spaces with a single pump room situated forward of the engine room. There was a separate piping system covering ballast pumps and lines

Supporting the cargo-piping diagram, the distribution of tanks can be clearly identified in this photograph of *British Tay*. The projecting conning station in the wheelhouse can also be seen. Roly Weekes.

This selection of the River class of BP tankers continues, with an imposing shot of the fourth ship, *British Trent*, taken in her final stages of discharge at Fawley Refinery, Southampton Water. This 25,550 sdwt vessel was a further delivery from Eriksberg's yards and was launched on 25 May 1973 with completion the following November. This ill-fated tanker became a casualty whilst on passage in dense fog from Antwerp to Fiumicino, the port of Rome, on 3 June 1993. She had just dropped her pilot and was still navigating Flushing Roads when there was a collision with the Panamanian bulk carrier *Western Winner*. *British Trent* had discharged part of her cargo but had not time to clean her tanks so was in a volatile condition. Ignition of hydrocarbon gas caused an explosion, but fire-fighting tugs eventually subdued the blaze and she was towed stern first to Rotterdam deep water anchorage for inspection prior to entering that port for completion of cargo discharge. On 10 June whilst berthed at Botlek Refinery in Rotterdam, the wreck was sold to the Dutch salvage firm Smit Internationale who towed it to Aliağa, Turkey, for demolition, where work commenced in September 1993. A sad ending for a magnificent tanker. N. Cutts.

British Avon was the first of four tankers in the River class constructed by Scott's Shipbuilding Company of Greenock, with other vessels built by British yards. She was 25,215 sdwt and was launched on 28 March 1972 for BP Thames Tanker Company and completed the following November. Her 6-cylinder oil engine was manufactured by the builders and developed 9,000 bhp, giving her a service speed averaging 16 knots on a laden summer draft of 31.4 feet. She served the company for 13 years, when in 1985 she was sold to Misano di Navigazione in Italy, who renamed her *Mare di Kara*. She had chequered ownership for the remainder of her trading. In 1987 the ship was sold to Trasporti Marittima Riuniti of Palermo who kept her for one year before selling her to Venezia Tankers who renamed her *Carnia*. This owner sold her in 1988 to another Italian ship owner, Starlauro of Naples, who called her *Laurotank Carnia*. The following year it renamed her *Carnia* and under this name she was sold to Feldene Shipping Company of Panama. It kept the tanker for three years before selling her on to Lefkaritis Brothers of Cyprus. In 1997 Dutch owner Columbia Ship Management was appointed as manager, but on 8 April 2000 she arrived at Alang to be scrapped. Roly Weekes.

The final ship in the class built by Scott's was the 25,551 sdwt *British Forth*. This product tanker was completed in December 1973 for BP Thames Tanker Company with whom she traded until 1990 when she was transferred to BP Shipping Company. In 1993 BP sold her to Maltese owner Camargue Shipping Company who called her *Camargue*, and appointed Arminter SAM to manage her. She is shown in this photograph off Valletta, stationary but with tugs fore and aft and other attendant craft. The year 2000 saw her sold to Therissos Shipping of Greece, who renamed her *Chryssi* and kept her for three years until selling her on to Palm Hellenic Navigation Company, Panama, who called her *Bedour*. Her future movements and eventual disposal from this date are uncertain. M. Cass.

EIGHT

BP Shipping Company's 1970s VLCC revolution

Alongside the company's growing fleet of product and dual-purpose carriers, the 20 VLCCs planned and ordered in the mid-1960s were gradually completed, and were launched over the next six years. Of this number, 15 would come from Japanese yards and 4 from Holland, whilst France delivered one. It rarely ceased to amaze non-seafarers that such massive ships, ranging between 250,000 and 500,000 sdwt, could operate with just 20 to 30 crew, depending on the number of junior engineer officers and deck/ engineering cadets carried for training. The increases in often quite sophisticated technology meant a reduction in the number of deck and engineering ratings required, whilst the term 'general purpose' implied a doubling of duties once the necessary training had been received, usually in sea schools ashore. Navigating officers suddenly found themselves taking advanced computerised radar, and a range of bridge technology courses, whilst improved deck techniques meant that 'more thought and less muscle' became increasingly important to mariners. Later, satellites would spell the demise of the radio officer's position aboard all classes of ship.

For BP, while the new generation of tankers meant an increase in tonnage, it also meant a reduction in the number of crude oil carriers. In 1965, for example, the company owned 120 ships totalling 3 million tons deadweight, whilst in 1974 it owned 97 ships with a summer deadweight tonnage totalling 6.8 million tons.

The first of the new VLCC buildings was *British Explorer* which was launched on 16 November 1969 from Mitsubishi Heavy Industries at Nagasaki for BP Medway Tanker Company. She was completed and sailed on her maiden voyage in March 1970.

Japanese yards were well experienced in VLCC construction, and progressively advanced technologically by 1970. As indicated from 'vital statistics' of the 346-metre (1,133-foot) length overall, 53-metre (174-foot) moulded beam, and 326,585 sdwt *Universe Ireland*, built by Ishikawajima-Harima Heavy Industries at its Negishi yards, the dimensions of these very large tankers were impressive. *British Explorer* at 215,603 sdwt and 108,530 grt was quite modest in terms of VLCCs, but she was still 326 metres in length between perpendiculars (as the British Merchant Navy adopted metric measurements) with a beam of 48.7 metres, and depth 20.7 metres. Similar to most ships of this class, she was powered by two Westinghouse-type steam turbine engines,

The appropriately named 215,603 sdwt *British Explorer* was the first of 19 VLCCs ordered by BP to serve various subsidiary companies under its wider umbrella. The 215,603 sdwt, 326-metre vessel was launched from the Nagasaki yards of Mitsubishi Heavy Industries for BP Medway Tankers, and served until 1976 when she was managed by the Irano-British Ship Service Company. She sailed with that company until July 1981 when she arrived at Kaohsiung for demolition. Here, she is shown made fast to a single buoy mooring, which soon became a popular alternative option for discharging crude oil. BP Plc.

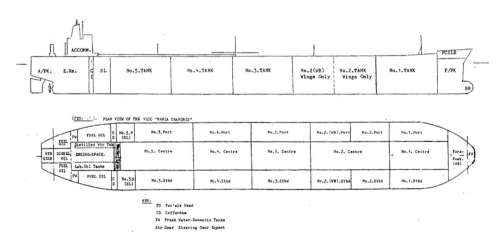

The general arrangement of a typical VLCC cargo and ballast tank configuration can be seen from this comparative elevation and plan. Whilst the details varied considerably between companies, the basic structure of five large cargo tanks with separate ballast tanks would be pretty much the same for the large BP tankers. There would always be a cofferdam between the engines and after slop tanks containing the pump room, with often a second cofferdam forward. Invariably in most unladen VLCCs, delegated centre tanks were available for additional seawater ballast in extreme weather conditions.

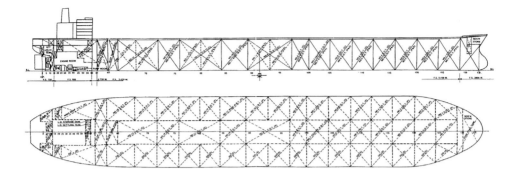

The plan and side elevation of ULCC *Jahre Viking* shows the tank configuration of this impressive tanker. Apart from the fore and after peak tanks, permanent water ballast was taken in Number 11 wings and Number 7 centre tanks.

manufactured in this case by the builders. Usually these were geared to a single shaft and developed around 30,000 shp, giving a charter service speed between 15.5 and 16.0 knots on a laden summer draught around 18.9 metres.

Most VLCCs had a similar cargo tank construction. Invariably the hull was divided into five centre and two wing tanks, but considerable variations occurred with the configuration of the wings. The Number 5 wings usually had the after portion devoted to slop tanks which accepted the oily-water cargo resulting from water-wash tank cleaning.

Chandris of England's *Rania Chandris* and Mobil Shipping's *Saudi Splendour*, with which I was acquainted, were similar in dimensions and tank configuration. Each had a deadweight capacity of around 286,000 tons with an overall length around 347.2 metres, with a moulded beam of 51.9 metres – dimensions that were marginally the same as the larger R class BP VLCCs. The largest tank was Number 2 Centre, at 63 metres in length and 21.7 metres wide. Number 2 Wings was divided into two equal parts, port and starboard, with the after section serving as water ballast. Number 2 Centre aboard the 1975 *British Reliance,* for example, was 62.7 metres long, with a capacity of just under 30,000 tons (the size of an average products carrier of the times), but the freeboard on all of these ships was around 5.7 metres.

The years 1973 and 1974 proved of considerable importance for BP's oil markets, but above all for international environmental protection and oil tanker safety. It was the size of supertankers and their massive cargo capacity that re-focused the world's attention on ever-growing problems that were arising from the contamination of the seas. In 1948, the United Nations had established the London–based International Maritime Consultative Organization (IMCO) as its agency with responsibility for all matters pertaining to shipping. The way it operated was by overseeing and implementing conventions and protocols through individual nations' flag states which established codes of conduct applicable to all signatories. Whilst IMO (as it became in 1954) had – and at the time of writing still has – no direct regulatory powers, its conventions and protocols remain incorporated into the national laws of all member flag states. It is open to them to take responsibility for legal enforcement. The organisation was formed specifically to introduce far-reaching regulations governing all aspects of ship safety, including load line, shipboard equipment including lifeboats, and tonnage control as well as attempting to deal with serious environmental issues arising from the oil pollution of the seas. Much later, IMO's remit would encompass wider concerns such as ballast water transference and air pollution.

The prevention of pollution by oil in the world's oceans had long been a major concern. The passing of the Oil in Navigable Waters Act by the British government in 1922, supported by subsequent work in this area by the United States, made early attempts to exercise at least a measure of control, but it was to take a major catastrophe before the minds of governments became really focused. As is well known today, the catalyst was the wreck of *Torrey Canyon* in 1967, followed all too soon by strandings of far too many large and very large crude oil tankers with disastrous damage to all areas of the environment, which had permanently serious and far-reaching repercussions. Gradually, rightful outcries from the world's media focused the minds of the public internationally, attracting widespread support and inevitably rousing and galvanising all maritime governments into action.

For the first time, in the mid-1970s zones were established in which it became illegal for any tanker to discharge oily waste accumulated from tank cleaning into the seas. But this was only the first step. Soon to follow were Marine Pollution Protocols under the collective heading MARPOL73/78. Among other considerations, this introduced areas aboard tankers designated as safe or hazardous zones. The accommodation block, including the engine room, were designated 'safe (or non-hazardous) zones', which had potentially flammable cargo vapour and sources of ignition excluded. A safety barrier was established and enforced which separated the hazardous area of the cargo main deck. Reinforced regulations were imposed that dealt with the safety of essential work that had to breach this area, such as on bunker fuel lines, cargo pump shafts, enclosed spaces, and other vital but sundry activity covering, for example, the fire mains, electrical conduits, cargo and temperature sampling points.

MARPOL73 was followed by 1978 Amendments, each ratified by all member states in those years with immediate effect even though, in keeping with all legislation requiring agreement internationally, the wheels had moved (and continue to move) very slowly, but extremely thoroughly. Just one IMO action, for example which affected all crude oil carriers was the introduction of a separate system for water ballast pumps and pipelines, whilst still permitting use of designated centre cargo tanks to take extra centre-tank ballast when facing extreme weather conditions.

IMO also confronted problems arising from the disposal of what could amount to 2,000 tons of oily-water mixture each voyage. This issue had remained very much an open question. Initially it was usual – and legal – for slops to be discharged into the world's oceans providing the tanker was at least 60 miles off any shore. Inevitably this caused considerable concern not only to environmental protectionists, but also to the more aware, and caring, masters and officers who found themselves responsible for doing the dumping. IMO solved this problem by encouraging shore refineries to accept the mixture, but later developments by Shell Tankers, which soon became internationally used, was their 'load on top' arrangement whereby the residue was retained on board and intermingled with the new cargo. There were no problems of contamination arising from the mixing of the various grades, as the comparatively modest quantities were soon lost in the hundreds of thousands of tons subsequently loaded.

The problem of limited draught alongside berths had been foreseen by BP. The remedies included extending jetties and dredging appropriate depths. Its new terminals at Grain, Finnart and elsewhere were foremost in this programme, with particular emphasis on Continental facilities, plus additional jetties elsewhere. As seen with *British Explorer*, single buoy moorings were established at ports with adequate crude oil capacity, helping overcome the problems of limited cargo-handling facilities in terms of jetties or docks, where these were located.

To assist deeply laden VLCCs to reduce their draught and safely navigate channels with restricted depths of water, a system of ship lightering was introduced. This enabled a smaller tanker, often between 50/60,000 sdwt capacity, to come alongside the VLCC and offload that amount of cargo. On passage from the Arabian Gulf or Nigeria to northern European terminals, for example, the ship-to-ship transfer would take place in the English Channel around 7–8 miles off Berry Head, on the east Devon coast, at the western extent of Lyme Bay. Both ships would proceed at a slow speed, the lightering tanker coming alongside the larger vessel and making fast to it. Once they were both in position, the VLCC would anchor. The operation could be carried out perfectly safely, even in the gale force 8 westerly winds frequent in this area, in the lee of the hilly shore. Upon completion, the lightering ship would cast off and both tankers proceed on passage.

In June 1970 the second VLCC, *British Inventor*, was completed and delivered from the same Japanese yards as *British Explorer*, with similar dimensions. It is fair to mention that those British yards which had proved themselves capable of building reliable and efficient VLCCs had been invited to tender for this new class of BP supertankers, but were unable to meet many of the conditions offered by foreign yards, especially regarding costs and reliable delivery dates.

The 52,928 sdwt tanker *British Dragoon* was completed at Hawthorn Leslie's yards at Hebburn in November 1963 for the BP Tanker Company. The ship continued regular trading until the advent of the VLCC class of crude oil carrier in the 1970s, when her capacity made her a useful lightering vessel to serve these larger-capacity tankers. *British Dragoon* was fitted with four foam-filled Swettenham fenders each about 4.5 metres in length and 3.3 metres in diameter. They were suspended on specially constructed davits enabling them to be raised and lowered like lifeboats. She was employed in this task until December 1982, when she was scrapped at Kaohsiung. Roly Weekes.

Seen just after being made fast alongside an unspecified BP VLCC, *British Dragoon*, towering over the main deck of the larger tanker, has lowered her midships derrick holding the connecting pipe. This is being made fast to the main cargo pipes; once connected, the pipe will be raised, taking the strain off the railings of both ships. Lightering was usually quite uncomplicated and proceeded smoothly, with the complete operation, from closing the lightering ship to casting off final warps, lasting around 12 hours. BP Plc.

British Inventor was a close sister ship to her predecessor, and was delivered from the same Japanese yards in June 1970, just three months after *British Explorer*. Her future followed a similar pattern, for she too was managed by the Irano-British Ship Service company and ended her days at Kaohsiung in July 1981. Viewing this vessel from the starboard quarter illustrates the complex dimensions and structure of these ships. For example, from the top of the funnel to the keel was 64 metres and to the bridge the distance was 50.3 metres. BP Plc.

BP's VLCC *British Pioneer* was also built by Mitsubishi, but came from its yards at Chiba. She was completed in June 1971 for Medway Tankers and transferred to the Irano-British management along with the other vessels. In 1981 she was sold to a Greek company, Tishpion Navigation, who renamed her *Tishpion*, and four years later she was resold to a Turkish concern who called her *M Cayhan*. It was whilst sailing with this company that she became involved in the Irano-Iraqi war whilst on a voyage, fully laden, between Kharg Island and the port of Sirri, in Iran. On 12 July 1985 she was again struck by Iraqi missiles when just 100 miles south of her departure port, and set ablaze. Two days later the fire was finally extinguished following sterling efforts by the ship's crew, but considerable damage had been sustained: her accommodation block and engine room were rendered almost uninhabitable, and tugs had to be called to enable her arrival at Sirri. She was anchored for a while before discharging her cargo, and eventually towed to Kaohsiung for scrapping. BP Plc.

The VLCC *British Navigator* was the last of the four contracted to Mitsubishi and was completed in its Nagasaki yards in June 1991 for BP Medway Tanker Company. In 1976 she was sold to National Iranian Oil and renamed *Sivand*. In October 1984, she too became involved in the Gulf War and suffered minor damage, but three days later, on 15 October, when loaded and plying between Kharg and Sirri Island, missiles from Iraqi aircraft set her alight. Her crew, too, extinguished the blaze, and she too ended her voyage under tow. In May 1986 she ended up for disposal at Kaohsiung. *The Motor Ship*.

In the after part of *British Navigator* pumps and pipelines have been lifted aboard and placed into position. The main cargo pipes are extended vertically, with crossovers enabling transference of cargo for loading and ballasting purposes. If you look closely, you may be able to discern the ant-like figures of the ship workers fitting the last stages to the port side pipeline, with another man aft of the starboard vertical pipe. BP Plc.

The following photographs of *British Navigator* and *British Inventor* indicate the construction of very large tankers. In Japanese and many European ship construction yards, units were built in sheds ashore and transported to the building dry dock, where the main sections of hull and accommodation block were assembled. They were lifted aboard by very heavy duty gantry cranes, after which the ship was towed to her fitting-out berth for completion. As conventional launching was totally impracticable with such large tankers, most were built in a dry dock that was flooded upon completion, the ship then towed to a fitting-out berth for completion. Some Dutch yards built their VLCCs in two halves and towed these to a dock for welding.

The tanker's after part having been completed, she is lying alongside her fitting-out berth. Propulsion provided by the engines deflected water and allowed this to flow laterally across the propeller and the rudder. The rudder would have been sited at a specific distance from the propeller, following the shore engineering superintendent's complex calculations, resulting in an efficient manoeuvring system. Most VLCCs had engines of around 30,000 shp, turning at around 86 revolutions per minute. This ship's engines consisted of two Westinghouse-type double-reduction steam turbines, manufactured by the builders, and geared to a single shaft. Some ULCCs and an occasional VLCC were constructed with two propellers, but this was not always successful, not only regarding costs but, as some pilots and those who sailed in them commented that under certain tidal conditions the ships were rather difficult to handle at very slow speeds. The propeller, the most expensive single item on the ship, would be fitted with between four and six blades, and would measure around 10 metres in diameter, and weigh 60 tons. A considerable number of these were made of nikalium (a nickel aluminium bronze alloy) by Stone Manganese Marine of Birkenhead and shipped across the world. The rudder, overcoming water pressure, was controlled and supported by a pintle working from a hydraulic motor system that enabled the ship to steer. Rudders were constructed around a network of highly reinforced vertical and horizontal frames, and were one of four different types, weighing around 200 tons. BP Plc.

Looking along the starboard side of the hull approaching completion. The single shell plating on VLCCs was made from mild steel around 20 mm thick, with extra strengthening of 27 mm at the keel plate. High tensile steel was not used until later in the 1970s, and generally then only at the bottom and deck areas. The advantages of HT steel were not only its cheapness but also its enhanced strength produced when under pressure, notwithstanding a slight reduction in weight. BP Plc.

The cargo centre tanks have begun to take shape, showing vertical and horizontal members. Whilst practices in shipyards varied considerably, basically centre tanks were the first to be constructed, with wing tanks added in sets with the progression of the hull along its length. The oil-tight transversal bulkhead between cargo tanks, again of *British Navigator*, is in position showing an array of brackets, stiffeners and transversal frames in the tanks immediately aft. BP Plc.

All centre and wing cargo tanks, plus the forward cofferdam, are completed, leaving the bosun's store and forepeak ballast tank to receive their strengthening prior to completion of the bulbous bow. BP Plc.

Looking forward, the main cargo piping can be seen in its final position, with work commenced to complete the manifold connections. The thinner pipes are part of the ballast line system. In *British Inventor*, the valves for both types of pipe were operated manually on deck from square boxes. Another 'ant-like' white-boiler-suited figure on the port side aft of midships emphasises the sheer size of cargo gear aboard these very large tankers. BP Plc.

The main deck is nearing completion, with centre-tank plating fixed and the wing tanks yet to be completed; the swash bulkhead construction in the wing tanks is clearly visible. The forward deck plating being lowered probably weighs around 120 tons, but these powerful gantry cranes with a safe working load (swl) of about 800 tons were perfectly capable of coping with such comparatively modest loads. The bulbous bow is receiving its final strengthening. This was set at an optimum depth to the hull of the ship, and deflects the downwards and outwards flow of water to create a secondary pressure system out of phase with the wave motion generated when the ship is under way. Note two other VLCCs in various stages of construction on either side of *British Inventor*. It was not unusual for work to be rolled over in this manner. The ship in the nearest building dock, very close to completion, is *James O'Brien* owned by the Chevron UK associate of this American oil major. She was 216,641 sdwt with an overall length of 326 metres. BP Plc.

Consistent with BP's new image, new streamlined funnel markings were designed, where prominence was given to the BP shield, significant on a white background set against the red black-topped funnel. This funnel was en route for fitting aboard *British Inventor*. BP Plc.

The completed VLCC *British Navigator*, ready to be launched and towed to her fitting-out berth. The function of the breakwaters aft was to deflect the heavy weights of water when the vessel was fully laden with a low freeboard, helping protect vulnerable crossover piping. The catwalk and fire monitors have yet to be added. BP Plc.

The fifth VLCC ordered by BP was the 219,994 sdwt *British Scientist*. Launched on 12 July 1971 at Kawasaki dockyard, Kobe, for Clyde Charter Company, she was completed for BP Medway Tankers the following October. The tanker was transferred back to Clyde Charter the same year, and remained with the fleet until 1981, when she was sold to Taiwanese shipbreakers. Roly Weekes.

On 8 July 1971 the 218,814 sdwt *British Prospector* was launched at Mitsubishi's Nagasaki yards. She was finished in November of that year, and served with BP Medway Tankers for the remainder of her service with the company. The vessel was sold to South Foundation Shipping of Liberia in 1979, who renamed her *South Foundation*, and with whom she spent her remaining sea time. In February 1983 the VLCC was sold for demolition in South Korea at Ulsan. Sensibly, BP corporate management sought best possible salvage terms from around the world for what amounted to 23,000 tons of scrap metal. BP Plc.

In the early to mid-1970s there was an international shortage of navigating and engineering officers across all types of ship. Tankers, especially the rising class of VLCCs, were hit particularly hard, so recruiting presented another (perennial) problem of ship management. For obvious reasons, the refineries were invariably situated miles away from places suitable for local leave and relaxation, so once the crew member was on ships' articles it was quite normal for them to postpone their leave until the termination of the trip – perhaps as much as six or seven months after signing.

In efforts to address these issues, reputable tanker companies had traditionally prided themselves on providing good standards of hotelier-style service for their officers and crews. This was reflected especially on VLCC class vessels, where catering rates were additionally generous, and great efforts were made to improve the living conditions. Double-bunked cabins were provided, enabling officers' spouses to accompany them, whilst en-suite facilities became the norm for even the most junior officer. Most ratings aboard VLCCs would have their own cabin, with mess rooms tastefully completed, often in blue Formica. Facilities on board assisting relaxation for all crew members received extra attention at the building planning stage, with gymnasia, games rooms and swimming pools soon becoming standard. But undoubtedly the greatest recruiting effect lay in the reduction of voyage lengths. While previously these had consisted of 'endless months' they were restricted initially for VLCC crews to specific tours of two voyages of around four to six months' duration, followed by one trip for leave. This pattern gradually became the norm for all men and women serving on the tankers owned by the oil majors.

The officers' smoke room for off-duty relaxation contained comfortable stools and a bar to give as close an impression as possible of a good public house or hotel ashore, notwithstanding the motion of the vessel on many occasions! Comfortable armchairs and decorated Formica bulkheads were the norm, with a steward regularly on duty at peak luncheon or evening hours, and out of hours the bar would be run by an officer who ran the company's signed-chit system. Ray Solly.

All chief officers' and second engineers' day rooms were conducive to helping the off-duty periods to be as relaxing as possible. One of the advantages of serving on a VLCC over a lower-capacity tanker was the spacious cabins not only for senior officers, but across all ranks. BP Plc.

The captain's and chief engineer's day rooms were often used for officers' regular meetings and pre-luncheon drinks for senior ranks, as well as entertaining countless port authority and other port visitors who had official business with senior ships' officers. Ray Solly.

The galley aboard VLCCs was large and spacious, making this area easy to keep clean, facilitating all stages of food production for the approximately 25 to 30 officers and ratings. Numbers were dependent upon the how many junior engineers were carried for training and assistance purposes, plus the number of deck/engineering cadets. BP Plc.

Service in the dining saloon was provided by stewards, who also kept the accommodation and cabins clean for their respective departmental officers. The captain's steward usually served the master and senior officers at their table, with navigating officers and sparks catered for by the officer's steward, and engineers by their own steward. BP Plc.

Very large tankers often arrived at their loading port to find it was necessary to anchor for a few days awaiting a berth alongside. This extra time was sometimes put to good use by off-duty officers who would lower one of the boats for relaxation purposes. Here an opportunity was taken by officers and crew serving aboard the 407,823 sdwt, 366-metre (1,200-foot overall) ULCC *Bridgetown*, either to 'exercise the engine, making sure it was running correctly' or to 'take the draught of the vessel'. Alternatively for the latter, a cadet or a deck boy would be lowered over the side by the stores crane. Both photos Captain 'Tinker' Taylor.

The wide main deck of VLCCs lent itself readily to games of cricket serving to reinforce the often strong bonds which would develop between officers and crews living in such close proximity aboard tankers. BP Plc.

Table tennis served as an opportunity for crews to exercise, as an alternative to using the equipment in the gymnasium or taking the main deck circuit four times, equivalent to a one-mile walk. BP Plc.

22 December 1971 saw the launch of the 222,745 sdwt *British Surveyor* from Mitsui Shipbuilding's yards at Ichihara, with her completion for BP Medway Tankers in March 1972. This vessel was the only one of her supertanker class to be delivered to the BP conglomerate in that year. In 1976 she was another VLCC sold to Iranian National Shipping Company who renamed her *Shoush*. On 29 August 1987 the ship became yet another company casualty in the Iraqi-Irani Gulf war, sustaining damage to the hull on her port side. On 31 August, whilst on passage to Dubai, she was again hit by an Iraqi missile, and anchored off Dubai awaiting repair. Upon her return to service she was anchored off Hormuz, then in 1986 was used as a storage vessel until her eventual demolition. BP Plc.

Once a cargo had been discharged, the Chicksan (a patent coupling) shore connections were severed and the tanker made ready for sea. Here, the crew of *British Surveyor* tighten the manifold connections and flake down the mooring ropes. A combination of wire warps and polypropylene ropes would be used, depending on tidal conditions off the berth; in some rivers the spring tidal current could ebb and flow at as much as 4 or 5 knots. BP Plc.

Arguably above all other safety designs ratified by IMO was the Inert Gas System (IGS). Many professional mariners consider this to have been the most important safety device installed and operated aboard crude oil tankers in the 20th century. Research involving a number of American and British owners had started as early as the 1920s but for various reasons its implementation had been shelved until interest was renewed following considerable damage to the environment and loss of life from 1970, caused by explosions aboard, and by accidents to vessels, including VLCCs, owned by other companies.

These incidents, with some loss of life, aroused renewed interest and a sense of urgency, with subsequent experimentation leading to many encouraging results from ships fitted with the new system. Possibly the safety factors and the lack of an explosion arising from a large tanker, the IGS-fitted *Energy Concentration*, provided conclusive evidence of the efficacy of the system; this 215,000 sdwt VLCC had experienced severe hull damage whilst discharging in Rotterdam in 1980. It was shortly afterwards that IGS became officially sanctioned, making the system compulsory for all tankers exceeding 20,000 tons capacity.

It is true to say that many VLCCs owned by reputable oil majors had been fitted with IGS many years prior to this, with BP remaining a leader in these experiments. It had been an explosion aboard *British Bulldog* in 1956, and a subsequent fire aboard *British Flag* in Swansea whilst she was discharging in 1965. This had led to the death of a crew member with another injured, followed the next year by an explosion whilst loading *British Crown*, that had focused company minds towards further investigations, encouraging BP to be the first oil major to fit the system to its ships.

Certainly, in any large crude carrier's cargo tanks a number of factors contributed to risk. The tested and approved explosive safety limits lay between 1 per cent and 10 per cent flammable limits of oxygen to hydrocarbons, outside which an explosion would happen. In addition, before a tank fire and probable explosion could occur there was an essential requirement for three elements – oxygen, a source of ignition, and a combustible material – in the correct proportions. In a crude oil tank empty of its cargo there was inevitably oxygen present plus hydrocarbon gas from the cargo. It soon became apparent that the source of ignition in these tanks came from static electricity generated by the very powerful cleaning machines essential to remove most crude oil remaining on the tops, bottoms and sides of the tanks once the cargo had been removed. The principle upon which the IGS worked was to exclude from the tank all traces of oxygen, the easiest component to remove.

Briefly, the system was built within two major areas. The first was located in the non-hazardous engine room, consisting of the plant used to clean and purify the gas, and the second was in the hazardous area on deck, to regulate safe delivery to the cargo tanks.

The following diagram and photographs show the basic principles upon which the IGS functioned.

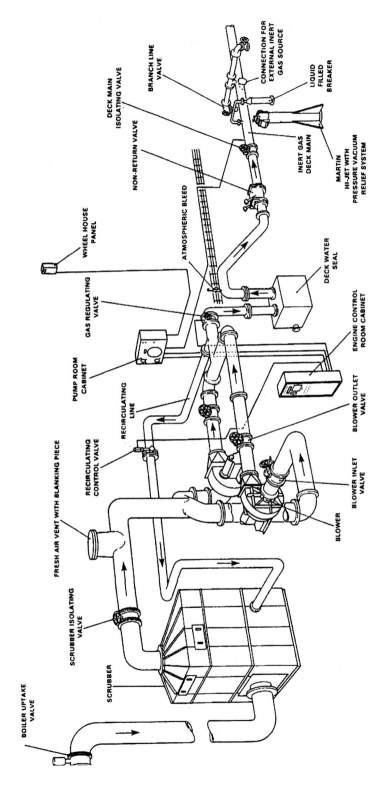

CONNECTION FOR EXTERNAL INERT GAS SOURCE

BRANCH LINE VALVE

LIQUID FILLED BREAKER

DECK MAIN ISOLATING VALVE

INERT GAS DECK MAIN

MARTIN HI-JET WITH PRESSURE VACUUM RELIEF SYSTEM

NON-RETURN VALVE

ATMOSPHERIC BLEED

DECK WATER SEAL

WHEEL HOUSE PANEL

GAS REGULATING VALVE

ENGINE CONTROL ROOM CABINET

PUMP ROOM CABINET

RECIRCULATING LINE

BLOWER OUTLET VALVE

FRESH AIR VENT WITH BLANKING PIECE

RECIRCULATING CONTROL VALVE

BLOWER INLET VALVE

BLOWER

SCRUBBER ISOLATING VALVE

SCRUBBER

BOILER UPTAKE VALVE

Schematic diagram showing an IGS aboard a BP tanker.

General view of the IGS plant aboard *British Explorer*. BP Plc.

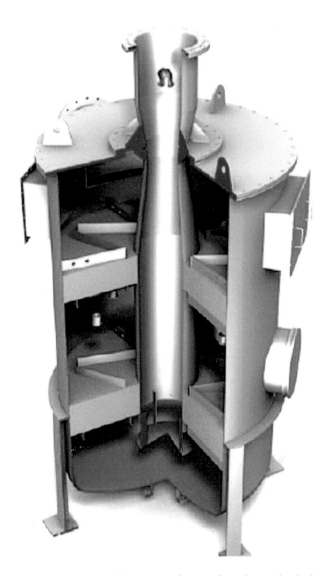

Plant in the engine room removed any remaining traces of oxygen from the gas that had passed through the ship's boilers. A remotely operated butterfly valve was fitted to the flue pipe at the base of the funnel, to draw off the hot exhaust. The gas – largely nitrogen, which would act as the neutralising agent against any remaining hydrocarbon gases – was wet, dirty and filled with solid particles of soot and other matter that required purifying after it had been cooled. This was achieved by feeding the gas into a scrubbing tower on deck, forward of the accommodation, where it was passed through a system of sprays, baffles and impingement plates to clean it and render it inert. This cut-away diagram of a scrubbing tower indicates how it worked. Aalborg Proactive.

The clean gas was then passed, under slight pressure from fan blowers, keeping it constant and stable, into a deck water seal. The image shows one of the two fan blowers usually aboard *British Explorer*. The seal was to prevent any backflow of flammable gas from the cargo tanks. BP Plc and Ray Solly.

After passing through a non-return valve, the gas passed into a main deck isolation valve. Its functions were to isolate the cargo tanks from the system and relieve any residual pressure when the system was not in use, for example whilst on a loaded passage. BP Plc.

The gas was then passed into pipelines leading to all centre and wing tanks. BP Plc.

There was always a risk in very large tankers that tanks could become over-pressured, so to prevent this a liquid-filled pressure breaker was provided. The gas, once expelled from the tanks, was led through purge pipes and high-pressure vacuum control valves fitted to the main lines. The pressure breaker consisted of an open-ended pipe running from the gas main into an inverted chamber open to the atmosphere at its upper end. It led to a riser fitted to the mast and (in those early days) fed the expired gas into the atmosphere. Ray Solly and BP Plc.

The clean gas supply could be topped up by a special IGS generator whenever appropriate during the ballast voyage, the entire IG system regulated from an operating panel (shown on the left-hand side) in the cargo control room. A number of safety alarms fitted into the system that would shut down the entire operation under certain dangerous circumstances. Ray Solly.

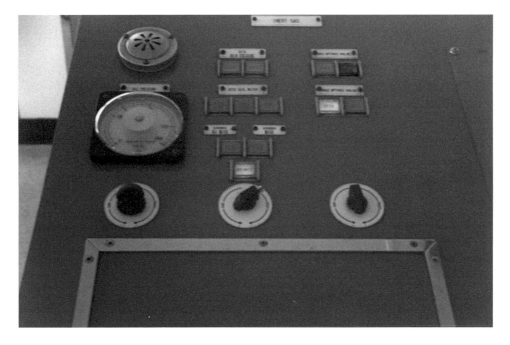

An IGS emergency control point was also situated in the wheelhouse. Ray Solly.

With the inevitable number of refinements introduced over the years, the IG system described still remains legally fundamental to all crude oil tankers in excess of 20,000 tons capacity, and has established its worth; correctly used, it has to date proved 100 per cent reliable.

~~~~~

In 1972, the Libyans took a leaf out of the Gulf's book by commandeering BP's interests in Libya – but far worse lay over the horizon, for the following year the international oil markets received a more devastatingly major commercial and political blow. Out of the blue, OPEC raised the price of crude oil to unprecedented levels, with an increase from US$2.90 to US$11.65 per barrel in a totally unexpected move, and at a time when demand was at its highest internationally. Not only were international oil and shipping industries affected but entire households worldwide suffered. This was not only from the inevitably massive increases in pump prices which followed as oil companies struggled to balance their books, but for some industry workers a three-day week evolved, with considerable loss of earnings.

The plummet in demand for oil had an immediate effect on the world's fleet of all classes and ranges of tankers that forced most shipowners unexpectedly to rethink where they stood as managers. Indeed, by 1975, tanker brokers estimated that around 466 tankers representing 37 million tons of shipping were laid up, with orders covering 174 tankers totalling 41 million tons cancelled, and a further 219 tankers representing 6.2 million tons scrapped. In some respects, this last move was not such a bad thing. For many years, crude oil tankers *per se* had, justifiably, received a pretty rocky press owing to unscrupulous shipowners who had run ships beyond the end of their useful lives with thinning rusty plates and indifferent crews. As the world now knows only too well, these had resulted in major oil spills, often with catastrophic effects on the environment, which damaged the reputation of the entire industry equally catastrophically. Reputable tanker owners were well served by the scrapping of such vessels and, importantly, IMO was given the green light to commence instituting moves that would eventually lead to rigidly tighter control of the offending flag states.

Inevitably BP Corporate, with its fleet of 92 tankers, was affected as hard as any other oil shipping major. Whilst delivery of the smaller River class of product tankers proceeded virtually unaffected, the contracts for the 19 VLCCs placed with various builders' yards were hit extremely badly, and 'the two flagships of the mid-sixties', *British Admiral* and *British Argosy*, were both scrapped at Kaohsiung within a couple of years. The machinations occurring in the boardroom cannot really be imagined or appreciated outside 'the circle', but the company directors quickly regained their equilibrium and with seasoned reason began reviewing how best this fleet of their ships might be pursued. This explanation suggests possible reasons why the apparent life of a VLCC serving the company during this decade or so has been seen to be so comparatively short. A potential 20-plus years' span of trading for each vessel became reduced to less than half of that time.

Delivery of the many company VLCCs close to completion continued, but inevitably some operating modifications occurred. *British Respect* was by this time well advanced in construction, and following delivery was immediately laid up in Brunei Bay, off Labuan. She was joined equally rapidly by *British Resource, British Purpose, British Prospector, British Progress* and *British Inventor. British Resolution* was converted into a storage tanker at Parita Bay in Panamanian waters, where she was joined by *British Renown.* Many of these VLCCs were to remain laid up for anything up to six years. By the end of 1974, many of the product and smaller dirty trade ships had also been laid up. *British Resource,* however, was converted into a motor tanker in 1981 and resumed successful regular trading until her demolition in 2000. But it would not be until December 1987 that all of the larger tankers were absorbed into regular service.

In other areas, moves were made attempting a re-negotiation of the contracts for the 14 VLCCs ordered with Mitsubishi Heavy Industries, but the penalties required eliminated this move as an option, leaving further behind-the-scenes inter-company machinations to be thought through that might ease the financial situation. For example, *British Rover* was completed as *British Norness,* whilst *British Ruler* became *British Trident,* both initially half-owned by BP and P&O, and eventually taken over by the latter following a successful 15-year charter. Ocean Trading Company, working with a comparative newcomer on the shipping scene, Airlease International, negotiated the conversion of two large tankers into four 20,000 grt dry cargo vessels, which were then absorbed into the Blue Funnel/Elder Dempster Lines fleet.

1973 was defined as 'not being a good year' for BP. The company's fortunes faced a further blow with the Kuwaiti government having decided to commandeer 60 per cent of the Kuwait Oil Company. Not to be backwards in coming forwards, the government returned the following year for the remaining 40 per cent. Its initial refusal to pay any compensation led to what were known in the trade as 'protracted negotiations', which eventually resulted in a $50 million settlement to BP and to Gulf Oil, the other company involved.

December 1975 saw the results of the company directors' deliberations; a major restructuring of the fleet emerged, streamlining the surviving tankers into three categories:

a. the crude oil fleet, which would consist of 29 tankers of mixed tonnage
b. a clean oil product fleet, which would total 35 vessels
c. a third fleet, which would contain a 'handy mix' of clean and dirty traders, around 16 ships.

The opportunity was taken of scrapping up to 25 older tankers, and the ownership of some associated groups of ships was rearranged with other companies. For instance, Common Brothers of Newcastle relinquished management of the Lowland Tankers, whilst the company's small coastal tankers run by Shell-Mex BP were either sold to other tanker owners or absorbed into wider company categories. Then, whilst retaining the BP corporate rights to its Norwegian sector of North Sea oil, interests were sold to the Norwegian government, for £27 million. Additionally, as it diversified, BP became the second largest chemical (including plastics and solvents) company in the world; it expanded its emerging information technological interests, which were by then being taken more seriously by all areas of society. It also invested widely in areas as diverse as animal breeding and feed interests, minerals and the coal industry.

As evidence that Fortune favours the bold, 1975 also saw the fruition of the investments BP had made five years earlier in its North Sea oil exploration at the Forties oilfield. The underwater wells began gushing, production at its peak over 500,000 barrels per day. This satisfied around 25 per cent of Britain's oil demands and, more importantly, offered at least a measure of independence from the politically uncertain Middle East fields.

Resuming the history of BP Shipping's fleet of VLCCs:

In 1971 the 260,905 sdwt *British Rover* had been ordered from Mitsubishi's Nagasaki yards by BP Medway Tanker Company. The contract was then sold, and on 15 June 1973 the vessel was launched as *British Norness* for Norcape Shipping Company (Bermuda) Limited based in London. The ship was placed on a 15-year demise charter with BP Tanker Company, who acted as operator and manager, and in September 1973 the VLCC was completed, to embark immediately upon her maiden voyage. 1981 saw BP Tanker Company as manager re-style its image as BP Shipping Limited (under which name it remains to this day), but the following year the ship was sold to Lombard Finance Company, also in London, although BP remained as operating manager. In 1986 the VLCC was transferred to the Gibraltar registry, with joint owners P&O, and two years later the same manager renamed her *Happy Norness*. Norman International A/S acted as manager to K/S Happy Norness Shipping, who bought the vessel in 1989. This company traded her for two years before selling on to K/S Thorness of Norway who renamed her *Thorness* and appointed A/S Thor Dahl Shipping as manager. In 1993 she was sold to Greek owner Symi Shipping Company, who promptly renamed her *Symi*, and in 1997 she was sold to EME Symi Shipping Company, also in Greece, who appointed a fellow country firm, Aelos SA, as manager. In February 2000 her chequered career ended ignominiously on the beach at Alang, where she was finally demolished. BP Plc.

British Norness, having discharged her part-cargo, is shown leaving the BP Isle of Grain refinery in Kent. Her 53.62-metre beam photographed from an attendant craft can be seen to maximum advantage. Note the wheelhouse windows are not visible, indicating that this class of tanker had a blind sector from the bridge extending ahead by the length of the vessel forward of the wheelhouse. In practical terms this potential deficiency was taken into consideration so did not present too many problems. BP Plc.

The onboard duties of officers whilst a VLCC was under way on passage were many and varied. Planning meetings between senior officers were held in the master's office or day room, and would often include contributions from the junior officers who might be directly involved in the exercise, duty or drill, such as a rescue operation from a tank anywhere on the vessel. BP Plc.

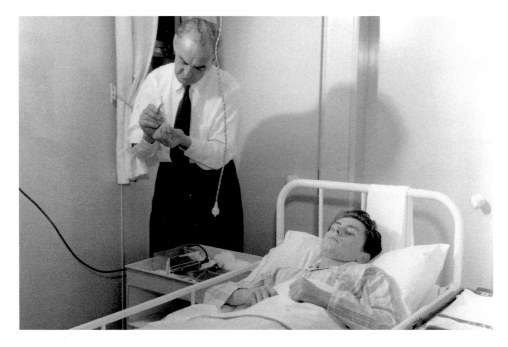

All officers had to hold a first aid certificate, usually issued on completion of a shoreside leave course held by the British Red Cross or St. John's Ambulance Association. The 'doctor' side of the practice was taken in the form of daily sick parades held by either the second officer or chief steward, with more serious cases admitted to the ship's hospital. Seafarers were generally a pretty healthy lot, but sometimes accidents occurred on board, or illness. Advice was often available by radio from port authority doctors' or ships with a surgeon on board such as a commercial liner, or a warship of any nationality. BP Plc.

The ninth VLCC owned by BP corporate, the 218,467 sdwt *British Pride* is shown leaving port. She was built at the Saint Nazaire yards of Chantiers de l'Atlantique, and launched on 16 June 1973, with completion for BP Thames Tanker Company the following October. In 1976 the VLCC was sold to NITC, who renamed her *Susangird*. She also became involved in the 1987 Iran-Iraqi war with serious consequences for the crew; on 9 December, on passage between Kharg Island and Larak Island also in the Gulf, she was attacked by Iraqi aircraft. The vessel was set on fire, and the following day the aircraft attacked her again, this time killing 21 of the crew. On 14 April 1988 she was repaired in Singapore, and she remained in regular service until beached at Alang in February 1995, where she was subsequently demolished. BP Plc.

Cadet training aboard BP tankers was always taken very seriously, and at varying times all deck officers became involved. As the youngest and most recently qualified officer, the third mate would have been nearest to the cadets' age, which would often allow greater degrees of relaxation in their relationship. In their early years cadets were usually placed in the wheelhouse for stand-by duties relating to entering or departing port; they were supervised in movement book entries, flags and the telephone. As they advanced in their training they would often be employed as quartermasters on the helm or in various capacities on deck; invariably the third mate would oversee these tasks. The second officer was responsible for the academic side of their studying, often directly supervising them for an hour per week on correspondence course progress and setting exercises on navigation or mathematics. These were completed by the cadets in their private study times and were often designed to correct detected weaknesses in written work. The chief officer was the cadets' direct working boss, responsible for all aspects of training, and often ran weekly meetings when, among other practical tasks such as rope work, the cadet was expected to learn one complete rule of the Collision Regulations, or a part of this. For their second mate's oral examination a thorough knowledge of these vitally important tools for ship-handling was expected, including comprehension of the implications of the 32 rules. All officers contributed towards helping the trainees in this vital task.

The second officer aboard *British Explorer* tests the cadet's understanding of the collision rule relating to vessels involved in the act of towage; the young person was expected to show detailed knowledge of the characteristics and range of each light displayed on the screen, and explain the action that they would take, or that they would expect to be taken by any target vessels. BP Plc.

The chief officer of *British Promise* offers instruction in the taking of bearings to one of the many female cadets recruited into the fleet from the mid-1960s. Many of the girls made successful careers with the company and in the Merchant Navy generally, with increasing numbers reaching command rank. BP Plc.

The master of a BP tanker checks a visual contact reported by the cadet; if it was another ship that had been detected, questions might well follow regarding the actions this target ship might take, bearing in mind existing circumstances and situations. BP Plc.

With her attendant support vessels surrounding her, and fresh from launching on 11 August 1973 from the Dutch yards of Verolme Dok & Scheepswerf at Rosenberg, the 253,839 sdwt *British Promise* is towed to her fitting-out berth for completion. This occurred in January 1974, after which she set out within a few days on her maiden voyage for BP Thames Tanker Company. In 1976 she was sold to INTC, and renamed *Sanandaj*. On 1 August 1986 she was used as a storage vessel, lying off the port of Hormuz for the best part of a year, and once she had resumed normal trading she became involved in the Iran-Iraqi war. She was attacked by Iraqi aircraft whilst loading at the offshore jetties of Kharg Island on 19 March 1987, and seriously damaged aft by fire, leading to the deaths of 26 of her crew, with only 4 rescued. Towed off the berth, she was later scrapped, and was deleted from Lloyd's Register sometime in 1994/5. C. van Noort.

British Promise is shown under way departing from an Iranian port with her pilot still on board and her gangway lowered above the boot topping to assist his departure. When VLCCs were first constructed they were fitted with a pilot hoist, but a number of accidents, culminating in the death of a pilot, led IMO to veto their use. The discolouration of the boot topping is not due to neglect, but arises from successful application of antifouling and anticorrosive paint, refreshed by the passage of the ship through the water. BP Plc.

Training was not restricted to cadets, as aboard ships of reputable companies once an officer had settled into their new routine they were invariably encouraged to take on at least some of the duties of the next higher rank. It was always reassuring for the new third officer, for instance, to discuss aspects of navigation or cargo and deck responsibilities. A third mate, on voyages subsequent to their first, could expect to be asked by the master to take charge forward on anchoring operations and, later, to assume complete control on the after deck on leaving port, and then on arrivals. The second mate would work closely with the chief officer on cargo work, especially planning loading/discharging duties and working the computer, helping assess limits of bending moments and various hull stresses.

The second officer on *British Promise* discusses a navigation aspect with the mate. Often the latter, on promotion, was responsible to the master for creating the voyage plan and arranging the appropriate chartwork – mindful, particularly on VLCCs, of water depths below the keel. BP Plc.

Second opinions were invariably welcomed regarding the actions of other vessels especially when these approached borderline situations, where perhaps the aspect of another vessel might cause some initial doubt regarding (for instance) whether or not it might be close to being in either an overtaking or a crossing situation. Once another ship had been detected, perhaps by radar, it was a reflex action to pick up the binoculars, to help determine if risk of collision existed. BP Plc.

The 224,989 sdwt VLCC *British Progress* had an interestingly unusual launch in that the ship, constructed by Nederlandsche Dok & Scheepswerf in Amsterdam, had her forepart launched on 24 February 1973 and her after part on 12 May of the same year. This practice seemed to be quite normal for the Dutch builders of these large tankers. The ship was completed the following October for BP Thames Tanker Company, with whom she served until scrapped in Kaohsiung on 5 March 1985. She is shown berthed in the Petroleumhaven 6e, Rotterdam. C. van Noort.

The third Dutch-built VLCC for Thames Tankers was the 228,600 sdwt *British Purpose*. She was built by the same Dutch yard, Nederlandsche D&S, in two parts, with the forepart launched on 11 August 1973, and the after part on 13 October. She was completed in March 1974 for BP Thames Tankers, with whom she served until demolished at Kaohsiung in February 1985. The ship is shown here commencing her maiden voyage in the Nieuw Waterweg. The boot topping makes an interesting comparison with that of *British Promise*. C. van Noort.

Interest is often expressed concerning the cargo tanks and routine deck duties undertaken whilst a VLCC is on passage at sea,. The following images show typical examples of essential equipment, and views rarely seen except by those serving on board.

A cargo pump on board *British Explorer*. These standard supply pumps were linked by a series of valves through a Centristrip system. Although variations existed, cargo discharge was usually governed by four turbine-driven pumps, each with an output of 2,750 hp at 60 bar steam pressure and a capacity of 3,500 m³/hr. Practically, each operated at a maximum discharge rate of 2,500 tonnes/hr and was fitted with a governor having a shaft speed ranging between 490 and 1,200 rpm. BP Plc.

The main cargo and stripping suctions within a cargo tank, showing the bell mouth situated about 17 mm from the plating to allow maximum suction. Ray Solly.

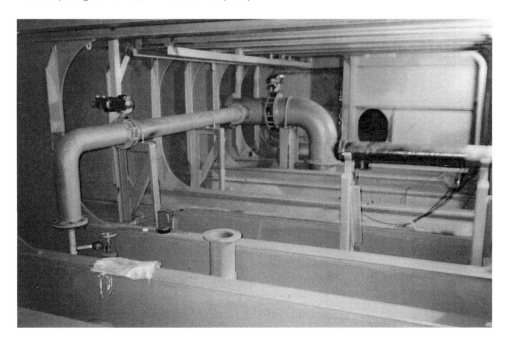

Ballast systems on all tankers were kept separate from the cargo lines. The turbine-operated pump generally ran at a speed of 6,500 rpm with an output of 1,250 hp giving an operating rate of around 250 tonnes/hr. The vertical stiffeners reinforcing the transversal bulkhead are clearly visible. Ray Solly.

Ballast tanks were originally fitted with sacrificial zinc anodes of the bar type, and coated to prevent corrosion; they were regularly inspected, with particular attention paid to the welding on seams and accesses. Tank entry was usually by a vertical ladder leading from/to a rathole on deck. Ray Solly.

Whilst the image of a navigating cadet transferring lifejackets aft depicts a routine task, the shot also shows from a unique angle, the vast expanse of deck from the fo'c'sle to aft of Number 2 cargo port tank – this distance representing just one quarter of the length of the entire main deck. BP Plc.

British Renown was the third tanker owned by BP Shipping; this 270,025 sdwt VLCC was launched at the Japanese yards of Mitsubishi in Nagasaki on 10 November 1973 for BP Thames Tanker Company. She was completed in 1978 and immediately converted into a storage vessel, but was reconverted into regular trading one year later to meet the fluctuations in demand for crude oil. On 10 July 1984, during the Iran-Iraqi war, whilst on passage to discharge the vessel *Tiburon*, she was attacked by Iraqi aircraft but the slight fire caused was extinguished by her crew. A day later she arrived at Dubai anchorage to have a one-metre hole in Number 2 starboard tank repaired. In September 1984 she sailed on passage to Gibraltar, and in 1985 was transferred to BP Thames Tankers. In 1990 she was transferred to BP Shipping Limited under the Bermudan register, with whom she served until scrapped on Gadani Beach in July 1994. BP Plc.

British Patience at 253,839 sdwt was another Dutch launch from the yards of Verolme D&S at Rosenberg on 22 December 1973, with completion for BP Thames Tankers the following May. This VLCC had a comparatively uncomplicated career, serving the same company until 27 October 1982, when she was demolished at Ulsan. Roly Weekes.

The 270,983 sdwt *British Trident* was completed at the Nagasaki yards of Mitsubishi on 4 June 1974 following her launch on 30 January of that year. This VLCC was built for Airlease International Nominees and leased to Charter Shipping Limited and P&O Bulk Shipping Division of London as manager, with an immediate 15-year demise charter to BP Tanker Company. In 1981 the charterers were restyled as BP Shipping Limited. For over three years, from 31 May 1983 until 9 July 1986, she was laid up at Brunei Bay until, under the same manager, she was renamed *Eastern Trust*. In 1990 the World Wide Shipping Agency of Hong Kong was appointed as manager, and it continued its duties until 1991, when the tanker was finally sold to Ritara Limited. The following year she was resold to Blue Wave Maritime SA of Panama and renamed *Assos Bay*. The career of the ship was further complicated when she was repossessed by United States Trust Company as mortgagees, then in March 1996, whilst continuing regular trading, she was renamed *Fortune Queen* and placed under the United Emirates registry. This lasted only a brief while, however, for on 1 April 1996 she was scrapped at Gadani Beach. BP Plc.

British Respect was launched by Kawasaki Heavy Industries of Sakaide, Japan, on 29 April 1974 for Scaledrene Limited of London, and completed the following September, with BP Tanker Company Limited appointed as manager. This 277,746 sdwt VLCC was the largest tanker associated with BP; in 1977 she was dry-docked, painted and dressed overall for the honour of representing this oil major at the Queen's Silver Jubilee Fleet Review, Spithead. In 1981 the manager was restyled as BP Shipping Limited, and in 1986 the ship was registered at Gibraltar. On 22 December 1987, whilst at Larak Island, she was attacked by Iraqi aircraft and set on fire. This was extinguished by her crew and under her own power she steamed to Dubai for repairs. On 4 February 1988 she returned to regular service, and in 1990 was transferred to BP Shipping and re-registered in the Bahamas. In 1992 she was sold to Delos Maritime Corporation of Greece, who renamed her *Delos*. She remained with associates of this company until her demolition at Chittagong in October 1999. Roly Weekes.

On 5 July 1974, the 270,665 sdwt *British Resolution* was launched by Mitsubishi's Nagasaki yards with completion for BP Medway Tankers the following November. Four years later she was converted to a storage tanker, and seven years after that was transferred to BP Thames Tanker Company who, the following year, returned her to regular trading. In 1990 she was transferred to BP Shipping and remained with the company until it was restyled BP Amoco Shipping Limited. The vessel was finally demolished later that year at Alang. BP Plc.

Mitsubishi's Nagasaki yards also launched *British Reliance* for BP Tanker Company on 23 May 1975, but this VLCC was completed in September of the same year for Crestaford Limited, with BP Tankers as manager. This 255,510 sdwt ship was then laid up for a year until September 1976, when she resumed regular trading under the same owner/manager. In 1981 the manager was restyled as BP Shipping Limited, and four years later the vessel sold completely to BP Shipping, who placed her under the Bahamas flag until the company was again restyled as BP Amoco Shipping Ltd. On 1 February 2000 *British Reliance* was anchored off the south China port of Zhuhai (opposite Macao) awaiting demolition. BP Plc.

British Resource was the 18th VLCC delivered. She was a near-sister ship to *British Reliance*, being 265,450 sdwt and was launched on 5 March 1975 for Erynflex Limited of London from the Nagasaki yards of Mitsubishi. She was completed in July of that year with BP Tanker Company appointed as manager. In 1976 the VLCC was transferred completely to BP Tankers and in April 1982 she was converted into a motor ship. In 1988 a transfer was made to Bermudan registry and two years later she was transferred to BP Shipping Limited. In 1999 the owner was restyled as BP Amoco Shipping Limited, with whom she served until demolition on 25 March 2000 by the Chinese Xinhui Ship Breaking Iron and Steel Company. World Ship Society.

The 20th, and final, VLCC owned or managed by BP was the 265,617 sdwt *British Ranger*. She too was a product of Mitsubishi's Nagasaki yards, who launched her on 23 August 1975 for BP Tanker Company. She was completed on 20 January 1976 for Solamole Limited with BP Tankers appointed as manager. Under BP Amoco Shipping ownership, she was scrapped in 2000. BP Plc.

Conclusion

For BP, 1975 was an instrumental year. It saw the eventual reopening of Suez, albeit with initial draught restrictions until the numerous wrecks blocking this important waterway were removed. Plans were also discussed within the Canal Authority to widen and deepen the canal, hopefully catering for the new breed of ever-increasing tonnage, thus enabling VLCCs to use it outward bound, at least, to the oilfields of the Middle East, even if the return had still to be made via the Cape.

It was around this time that the Iranian government, seeing the success of the Kuwaitis, also investigated the idea of flexing its muscles. BP stepped in quickly, so that it could at least have some say in these proposed moves, and it succeeded in forming the Iran-British Shipping Company Limited with the Iranian government, each with a 50–50 holding. Another shrewd move incorporated BP's third-category fleet, joined by a number of its tankers to be chartered to the new owners. This third fleet was eventually sold outright to the Iranian government's new shipping company, National Iranian Tankers, with these ships renamed and integrated, with a number of other tankers, into a mutual pool of operations.

We have seen that the black year for international shipping was 1945, with the ending of hostilities. This forced assessments of the situation and it determined essential plans regarding the future. Many shipowners of all classes of vessel worldwide went out of business, whilst others had to make reasoned decisions whether or not to try to effect a recovery.

BP had lost almost 50 per cent of its tankers, along with 673 seafarers lost in action or from the direct effects of their war service. This does not include those who died later of their wounds, nor the countless many who endured lifelong suffering, both physical and psychological. This drastic loss of personnel was reflected throughout the Merchant Navy, whose collective losses totalled over 36,000 officers and ratings. Inevitably, a refocusing on the recruitment of personnel became an immediate priority, together with replanning of training methods for officer cadets, apprentices and ratings. The existing fleet of tankers was old, with the youngest having seen 14 years' service, and all ships having received just minimum repair during the war years. On the positive side, things in the boardroom had not stood still, for already 11 tankers had been built prior to 1945, with another 8 launched during that year and, continuing this spirit of determined optimism, orders were placed with British yards covering a range of new-build tonnage. The existing fleet of 49 ships was systematically dry-docked, surveyed and repaired as necessary, and to provide continuity they were joined by 10 of the versatile class of T2 American tankers.

New buildings continued at an impressive rate throughout the 1950s, with new associated companies formed and alliances created designed to consolidate future plans. For instance, in 1952 the Lowland Tanker Company was launched on the Stock Exchange as a joint venture between Common Brothers and Mathesons, with BP holding the majority of shares and the other two companies joint equal partners. A total of 15 ships of 20,000 sdwt would eventually see service, although BP did not take over the complete management until 1976. A new company, Tanker Charter Limited, was formed to manage many of the new buildings which were joining an ever-growing fleet. Warwick Tankers was formed in 1958, its two 32,000 sdwt vessels owned jointly with Houlder Brothers. This latter company already had a large fleet of dry cargo vessels, along with a number of tankers in its own right. The Danish company East Asiatic, also owner of a large fleet of dry cargo ships, chartered two tankers to BP for periods extending up to ten years, whilst an offshoot Danish firm was created, called Nordic Tankships, which chartered a further two vessels.

The 1960s saw the launching of *British Kiwi* at 16,183 sdwt whilst the decade ended with *British Fidelity*, 24,414 sdwt. In between, the company launched 48 ships including, of course, the 112,000 sdwt *British Admiral* and *British Argosy*. The first of the VLCC class tankers, *British Explorer*, heralded the 1970s, with a further 21 tankers of all classes launched before 1975, completing with the *British Resource*.

In many respects the planned truly golden years for BP Corporate ended in 1973 with OPEC's decisive raising of oil prices to unprecedented levels. This gave little good news on the shipping front for the remainder of the decade until new strategies could fire into place. Most of the new VLCC fleet was laid up, and many other BP tankers were seeking the fuel oil and product markets which remained essential to the continuance of the ordinary processes of 20th century life.

But like many occasions where circumstances in life hit a negative, the devastating oil and shipping news produced promising signs across another associated area that, although not providing totally 'golden years' at least offered a fair measure of compensation. The increase in oil prices had a positive as well as negative effect, for the considerable resources in which BP had invested previously in its North Sea Forties oilfields and Prince Edward Sound in Canada increased enormously: sufficiently to help keep the corporate ship on an even keel.

There remains another less prosaic reason for company survival, one that resides beyond mere optimistic resilience, which can justify the decade as a collective golden year; the company possessed an invaluable asset far removed from tangible compounds such as ships and oil. For, from the days of the enterprising Edward d'Arcy who had set the Anglo-Iranian ball rolling in the early 1900s, the BP board of directors was capable of rising to meet the new challenges emanating from the difficult years of the 1970s. Throughout the long history of the company there is ample evidence that its senior management remains carefully recruited and tested (rightfully so), before selection. The process has to be self-perpetuating, for the people doing the recruiting remain those who were themselves recruited at earlier stages in their careers. Both successful job applicants and those who have been head-hunted are recognised as possessing proven intellectual ability, supported by equally proven aptitude across the company's range of requisite managemental areas. It was (and remains) perfectly possible for ordinary company employees who have shown above average intelligence and good sound common sense, combined with potential for entrepreneurial acumen, to rise to the board. I know personally of at least three such men who came from humble navigating officer cadet backgrounds, who showed potential by rising to command at a comparatively early age, who were then recognised and tested, and who ended their days serving the company in this top capacity. BP management also came (and doubtless continues to come) from a different sector of the social scale from its seafaring officers: the management are often promising academics graduating from top universities across the range of requisite areas who have neither served on a ship in their lives nor have any desire to do so – nor, indeed, any need to do so.

It would be true to say that this proven strategy continues, resulting in an effective company that continues to grow even greater in international prestige and bound inevitably to remain strong.

Select bibliography

Bamberg, J.H., *British Petroleum and Global Oil: The Challenge of Nationalism 1950–1975*, CUP, 2000

Ferrier, R.W., *The History of the British Petroleum Company*, CUP, 1982

Harvey, W.J. and Solly, Dr R.J., BP *Tankers: A Group Fleet History*, Chatham Publishing, 2005, (2006)

Lloyd's Register of Ships, Various editions

Middlemiss, M.L., *The British Tankers*, Shield Publications, (1989), 1995

Newton. J., *A Century of Tankers*, Intertanko, 2002

Smith, A., (Managing Editor), *Riding the Waves: BP Shipping 1915–2015*, BP Shipping Limited, 2015

Solly, Dr R.J., *Nothing over the Side; Examining Safe Oil Tankers*, Whittles, 2010

Supertankers: Anatomy and Operation, Witherby & Co., 2001

Various magazine editions:
BP Shield
The Motor Ship
Shipping and Transport
Tanker and Bulk Carrier
Tanker Times
Tanker Operator

Ship index